THE MODERN BUDDHISM AND ITS FOLLOWERS IN ORISSA

THE MODERN BUDDHISM

AND ITS

FOLLOWERS IN ORISSA

By

Nagendra Nath Vasu

Introduction By

Mahamahopadhyaya Haraprasad Shastri

GYAN

The Modern Buddhism
and its Followers in Orissa

Nagendra Nath Vasu

ISBN : 978-81-212-0057-8

First Published 1911, reprint 2013 in India by
Gyan Publishing House
23, Main Ansari Road, Daryaganj,
New Delhi - 110002
Phones : 23282060, 23261060

Fax : (011) 23285914
E-mail: books@gyanbooks.com
website: gyanbooks.com

Printed at : Sagar Color Scan, New Delhi.

PREFACE.

In November 1908, I was required to accompany the Feudatory Chief of Mayūrabhañja on an Archæological tour in the interior of his territories. We paid a visit to Khiching, which was once an important seat of the Bhañja Rājās. I mixed with the humble people of the neighbouring villages, and from this close contact with them observed some curious customs and manners amongst them which bear little affinity to those of the Hindus. At this stage a band of merry lads of the Pān caste entertained me with their songs, which were all upon the texts of the Dharmagītā. The songs interested me very much, as in the texts I found distinct indications of the tenets of Mahāyāna Buddhism. Shortly after this I met some old men, who recited the songs of the Pāla Kings of Bengal. These also belong to the period of the Buddhistic ascendancy. I was now convinced that Buddhism was not altogether a lost religion in Orissa. My curiosity being thus roused, I hunted after and soon laid my hands upon some old Oriyā MSS. which proved that Buddhism flourished in this part of the country so late as the 16th and 17th centuries. I now studied with care the sacred books of the Mahimā-dharmists and some other sects, who inhabit Khiching and various parts of Keonjhar, Dhenkanal and other gaḍajāts; and found that these people unmistakably profess Buddhistic tenets inspite of their not being recognised as Buddhists by the people. In comparatively recent times there has been a revival of this school of Buddhism.

The subject of the book has already been incorporated in my Mayūrabhañja Archæological Survey Reports, Vol. I. I now publish it separately with a preface by Mahāmahopādhyāya Haraprasād Shāstri M.A., whose researches in this direction 20 years ago brought to the notice of the world for the first time, the existence of Buddhism in modern Bengal. My researches and the results attained thereby only substantiate and supplement his theories and conclusions arrived at from a different stand-point. My grateful acknowledgements are due to him not only for the learned introduction with which he has embellished this treatise, but for the light which his original researches threw on my subsequent work in the same field.

I have also to express my indebtedness to H. H. the Chief of Mayūrabhañja. Without his aid and encouragement it would have been impossible for me to conduct these arduous researches in the jungly tracts of Mayūrabhañja.

I am also thankful to my friend Babu Dinesh Chandra Sen for his ready suggestions whenever I have had to consult him.

Since writing the book, I have come in possession of a number of Oriyā MSS. which elaborately prove the facts to be found in this book. If a second edition is called for, I shall incorporate these in the book next time.

VIÇVAKOSA OFFICE,
20, Kantapukar Lane, Bagbazar,
Calcutta, June 21st, 1911.

NAGENDRA NATH VASU.

CONTENTS.

INTRODUCTION.

'Çaŋkarāchārya drove away Buddhism from the soil of India'. This was the verdict of historians, sixty years ago. Buddhism—the religion of over forty per cent of the entire population of the world, professed in all countries, in the north, east and south of Asia,—was swept away from its birth place by the exertions of one single individual!

These historians, however, plainly contradicted themselves, for when they said that, 'Çaŋkarāchārya drove away Buddhism from the soil of India,' they also said that the Pālas, who reigned in India in the 9th and 10th centuries were Buddhists. This is a pure contradiction for no body ever imagined that Çaŋkarāchārya flourished after the fall of the Pāla Dynasty.

The sixties and the seventies were periods of the greatest activity for Archæological researches under Sir Alexander Cunningham. His researches, his excavations, and his discoveries all over Northern India, showed in unmistakable terms that Buddhism lingered in many parts of Northern India for hundred years after the Muhammadan conquest.

From the early eighties commenced the minute and scholarly investigations in all matters that related to India, both in Europe and in this country. The credit of initiating this accurate and sympathetic movement belongs to Hofrath Bühler. He and his numerous followers investigated very carefully all the available sources of information about India and then pronounced their opinions. The late lamented Prof. Bendal examined the wonderful collection of Palm-leaf Mss. in the University of Cambridge and found that many of them belonged to the Pāla period. Babu Çarat Chandra Dās travelled in Tibet and showed from Tibetan sources that a large number of Pandits, especially, from Eastern India, went to Tibet in the Pāla period.

Amongst other facts that were brought to light, the chief were that ;—a Buddhist temple was erected at Çrāvasti in the year 1276 A. D.; Buddhist priests from Tamluk went to the Pagan and reformed the Buddhist church there; the Budh-Gaya temple was repaired by the King of Burma in 1331 A. D.; Buddhist books were studied in Bengal even by Brahmins in the earlier years of the 15th century; Buddhist books were copied for Buddhist priests and laity during the middle of that century; about the end of the century a Bengali Brahmin of the Kātyāyana Gotra who was expelled from his country for his Buddhistic tendencies, was made Bauddhāgama Chakravarti in Ceylon and a biographer of Chaitanya said that at the birth of the infant God, Buddhists rejoiced greatly.

So traces of Buddhism in Eastern India were discernible up to the time of Chaitanya *i.e.*, the early part of the sixteenth century.

About the end of the sixteenth century Lama

Tāranātha, sent emissaries to India, to examine the state of Buddhism in that country. These reported that Buddhism was still to be found in Orissa and Western Bengal. But where is all that Buddhism gone ?

The Muhammadan historians never speak of Buddhism ; the historians of Mughal period do not even know its name. The historians of the British power in India, refers but scarcely to Buddhism. Where is all that Buddhism gone ?

Yuan Chuang tells us that there were ten thousand Saŋghārāmas with hundred thousand Bhikṣus in Bengal. To support this vast mendicant population at least ten millions of lay families were required, and they would be all Buddhists. The Chinese pilgrim further says that there were also heretics in the country, by which term he means the Brahminists and the Jainists. The number of Brahminists in Bengal was very limited. The Jains never made Bengal their stronghold. More than three-fourths of the population of Bengal were Buddhists.

Full one hundred years after Yuan Chuang, the original five progenitors of the present Rāḍhiya and Vārendra Brāhmans in Bengal came from Kanoj. Their religion was not a proselytising one. In the middle of the twelfth century Ballāla Sena took a census of the descendants of these five Brahmins and he found only eight hundred families in all. They lived mostly on grants of lands made to them by the Rājās or by fees for services rendered to the State. Servants and maid-servants were supplied to them by the

State. They practised their own religious rites with pomp and grandeur befitting their position as well-to-do men. But they rarely interfered with other people's religion. History tells us of defections from their ranks but of no additions to their strength. The masses were almost entirely left in the hands of the Buddhist priests, both married and unmarried, and there is reason to suppose that the married priests predominated in number. But the monastic orders were rich and powerful. They were very learned and their schools and colleges were celebrated all over the Buddhist world. The Monastaries of Nālanda, Vikramaçila, Jagaddala and other places were the best seminaries for the diffusion of Buddhist learning and Buddhist religion. It was from these monastaries that Tibet, Burma, Ceylon and Mangolia received their Buddhist preachers and Buddhist authors and translators.

But there were the married priests who officiated in the religious ceremonies of their lay brethern; these composed the litergy, worshipped Bodhisattvas and Gods, and officiated in marriages and funerals. They gradually introduced mantras or set formulæ for every religious ceremony and called this cult, Mantrayāna.

The word Mantrayana requires an explanation. People are familiar with the terms Hīnayāna, and Mahāyāna, but not with Mantrayāna. Hīnayāna, though a proselytising religion, concerned itself only with moral training and moral regulations, and thought only of individual salvation, while

Mahāyāna embodying the highest and noblest truths of philosophy and religion, extended salvation to all classes of men and like the Theosophists of the present day, comprehended within its fold men of all shades or opinion and faith. But is it possible for ordinary people to comprehend the noble truths of philosophy which required close study for years? Certainly not. What sort of Mahāyānists were the ordinary people then? These implicity believed in the superior talents of their masters, followed the course of conduct chalked out for them by them, repeated the vows and hymns which appeared most sacred to them, and studied the short works called *Dhāranis* invoking the spirit of Buddhas and Bodhisattvas and of the truths formulated in standard philosophical and religious works. There are more than six hundred Dhāraṇīs extant. The higher and more ancient class of these gives the pith of the noble works produced by the masters. But the lower and more modern class of these invokes the protecting Bodhisattvas and guardian deities for the attainment of worldly objects.

Gradually the language of these Dhāraṇis became antiquated, and difficult of comprehension, so Mantras were substituted for them. They were something like algebraical expressions of the Dhāraṇīs. How the Mantras were formed from the letters of Indian alphabets is a curious study by itself. It would be out of place to speak of them here. The Mantras were given to the ignorant laity. The repetition of the Mantras was considered equally efficacious with the study of the deeper problems of life. This is Mantrayāna. Yuan Chuang saw little of it in India in the 7th century. It flourished in the subsequent times. Then it was superseded by another and more attractive form of religion, half mystic, half philosophical and more sensual, than the previous forms of Buddhism. This is called Vajrayāna

How Vajrayāna arose from Mahāyāna is clearly indicated in the works of Vajrayāna literature. The human soul bent upon the attainment of the highest knowledge progresses from the lower regions of earth to the higher, till all flesh disappears and it rises above the world of *Kāma* to the world of *Rūpa* or form. The mind bent upon Bodhi passes on through a variety of forms till it reaches the highest of the *Rūpa* heavens, still Bodhi is not attained. It goes higher and higher to the region where form does not exist. This is called the Arūpaloka or the formless world. In its progress higher and higher in this formless world it rises to the top and vanishes in the infinite void. That is the idea of Nirvāṇa of the Mahāyānists, but the Vajrayānists at this stage mystically conceives the existences of Nirātmā Devī at the top of the formless (Arūpa) heaven. She seems to all intents and purposes a metaphor for the infinite void. From the top of the formless world the mind bent on Bodhi leapes into the embrace of Nirātmā Devī and enjoys something like the pleasures of the senses, and disappears in her, as salt disappears in water. Thus Vajrayāna is a curious mixture of mysticism, philosophy and sensuality. The sensual part of this doctrine made it exceedingly attractive and soon superseded the dry Mantrayāna and the difficult Mahāyāna.

In a work entitled Adikarmarachana by Tatakara Gupta, embodying the doctrines of Subhākara Gupta, a distinguished professor of the Vikramaçilā monastery we find a complete account of the daily duties of a Buddhist of the Mantrayāna school. In that book we are told that Mahāyāna has already become one of the Sikṣā-padas or vows or sacraments. It is no longer the school of philosophy studied with care for years but a set of religious ceremonies by which in a moment all the benefits of that patient study are supposed to be attained. Mantrayāna too has become a sacrament. This book was written in the ninth century A.D. or earlier. In modern times the Nepal Vajrayānists (none of whom lead a monastic celebate life), considered Vajrayāna to be the last sacrament after which they can seek female company for the practice of religion. They do not call it marriage exactly, but something like taking a *Cakti*. From the sketch given above, it will be seen how in India the great religion of Buddha rose to the soaring height of metaphysical speculations and how the necessity of keeping within its fold a vast number of ignorant lay people made it climb down to the Dhāraṇis, to the Mantrayāna, and to the Vajrayāna. The spread of the religion to people of even lower strata brought in the Kālachakrayāna. Dr. Waddel considers Kālachakrayāna to be prior to Vajrayāna, but this is opposed to all Indian tradition. The Nepal Buddhism, as apart from Lamaism, is still

Vajrayāna in the main, having only a small sprinkling of Kālachakrayāna. But what is Kālachakrayāna? The word Kāla means time, death, and destruction. Kālachakra is the wheel of destruction, and Kālachakrayāna means the vehicle for protection against the wheel of destruction. Waddel describes this as demonology, or devil-worship, and so it is. Even Buddha is a demon, and in the Asiatic Society's library there is a book entitled Buddha-Charita which describes Buddha as demon. Though the book was written in Ferok Shere's time at Benares, it certainly embodies much older tradition. Bibhūti Chandra of Jagaddala Vihāra who was a great master of Kālachakrayāna, flourished in the 13th century. Unless Buddha was mentioned in Kālachakrayāna, one would be inclined not to call it Buddhism at all.

Thus we have briefly indicated how Buddhism degenerated, from its great philosophical and speculative height, even to demonology. But there were other forms of religions which the Buddhist community gradually absorbed within itself. One of these is the Nāthamārga or Nāthism. The leaders of this sect were Nāthas who practised a form of Yoga much inferior to that taught by Buddha or by Patañjali, both of whom considered the concentration of the mind to one definite point as the chief process to attain salvation; but the Nāthas tried to restrict the internal air and to lead it from what they called Mūlādhāra below the abdomen to the forehead, and attain success (Siddhi) in the world rather than salvation. Many Nāthas are mentioned. They are also called Yogis. They came from outside Buddhism ; one of the principal Nāthas is Matsyendranātha or Machchhaghnapāda. A book attributed to him has been found written in the 10th century character. It is not a Buddhist book, yet Machchhendranātha is worshipped as an incarnation of Avalokiteçvara at Pātan ; the Buddhists of Nepal all attend the festival held in his honour. A Machhaghna or fisherman cannot be a Buddhist because he is a habitual animal-killer and Tatakara expressly excluded Kaivarttas from the pale of Buddhism. Thus the Nāthism of Matsyendra arose outside Buddhism, but was at last absorbed into it. On the other hand Ramaṇa-Vajra was a Buddhist of the Vajrayāna school, but when he became a Nātha, he became Gorakṣanātha, and was regarded as a heretic by Buddhists, so Gorakṣa's Nāthism was originally within Buddhism, but it was not incorporated into it. It is said that of the seven Nāthas, Gorakṣa was the only heretic.

In the 9th century sprang the sect of Sahajiyās who made salvation easy by reaching it through carnal enjoyments. How the sect arose is lost in obscurity, but it had so many features common with Vajrayāna, that it soon became absorbed in that system. The Sahajiyās found the great world *i. e.* the universe within the human body.

A great Sahajiyā exponent in Buddhism was Kṛṣṇāchārya or Kānhu who wrote both in Sanskrit and in Bengali. He is still worshipped in Tibet as a great wizard with a bald head and a flowing beard. Another exponent of the Sahajiyā sect of the Buddhist school was Lui, who is mentioned in Nagendra Bābu's "Modern Buddhism." His Bengali songs have been recently discovered, and goats are sacrificed to him in the Rāḍha country at the worship of Dharma on the fullmoon day of Vaiçākha. There are many other Sahajiyās who are worshipped in Tibet.

The Sahajiyās had three different ways of salvation, the Avadhūtī-mārga, the Cāṇḍālīmārga, and the Ḍombīmārga. In the Avadhūtī-mārga, the idea of duality is predominent. Avadhūti, though she lives apart, still mixes with people and therefore represents duality. The Chāṇḍālī lives apart but she has a community to mix with. She is therefore not so strong a represantative of duality as Avadhūtī, but she is not yet absolutely one. But Ḍombī lives far away from the inhabited locality and has no society. Therefore to a Sahajiyā to go to the Ḍombī means to be absolutely undual.

TANTRA:—The word Tantra is very loosely used. Ordinary people understand by it any system other than the Vedas. But it really means the worship of Çakti or Female energy. The female energy is worshipped in conjunction with male energy. The union of male and female energy is the essence of Tantra.

Tantra came from outside India. Most likely it came with Magi priests of the Scythians. In the old Saṁhitās such as Niçvāsatattva Saṁhitā, a wonder is expressed at the novel mode of initiation enjoined by the Tantras. Vedic initiation was known, but people wondered how could there be a new initiation other than Vedic. It came from outside India and spread on the outskirts of the Aryan world. The five original places of Tantra in India are Jālandhara, Punā, Çrīparvata, Oḍiāna and Kāmākhyā.

The Çakti-Saŋgama Tantra, a later work, declares that the object of that Tantra is to root out Buddhism and establish Brahminism, while Buddhist Tantras equally denounce Brahminism. The theory was current twenty years ago that the Brahmins derived their Tantras from the Buddhists, but of late it has been ascertained that neither did the Buddhists derive their form of Tantra from the Brahmins nor the Brahmins from the Buddhists. Both received their Tantras from the same source. But it spread more rapidly among the Buddhists than among the Brahminists. A popular religion like that propounded in the Tantras cannot but be attractive to the masses in Bengal and in Eastern India, where Buddhism prevailed. The Buddhist priests, especially the married classes, were not slow in taking advantage of this new form. The Tantras did not at first spread much among the Brahmins and their followers. It became in fact a recognised initiation only in the sixteenth century, and even then it was regarded as a subsidiary initiation designed more for the women and the Çūdras who had no claim to the Vedic initiation. Practically the prevalence of the Tantric rites among the Brahminists was conterminous with the total disappearance of Buddhism. Even in the very best of the Hindu Tantras we find the worship of many Bodhisattvas and gods and goddesses of the Buddhists. Mañjūçrī of the Buddhists is worshipped as Mañjughoṣa. Akṣobhya of the Buddhists is regarded either as a form of Çiva or a Ṛṣi to whom the Tārā-mantra was revealed. Ekajaṭā and Nīla-sarasvatī was bodily taken from Buddhism. The Bhūta-ḍāmara Tantra mentions the Bodhisattavas as objects of worship. One of the Hindu Tantras says that Vaçiṣṭha was anxious to attain success or Siddhi in the Tārā mantra, but failed to do so in India. He had to travel all over the snowy mountains to China, where Buddha taught him how he could be an expert in that mantra. The Tantras, many of them at least, discard all the āchāras prescribed by Brahmins and enjoin the āchāras of the Chinese. Even now the Tantric deities prefer to be worshipped by the lower castes than Brahmins. In many localities Durgā is worshipped first by the untouchable classes and then by Brahmins. Brahmins have to wait in some villages till the Pūjā has commenced at some Hāḍi's house in the neighbourhood. The Jayadratha-yāmāla says that the Devī likes to be worshipped by the oil-pressees; the Tailakāras. Three men in the sixteenth century and one man in the seventeenth made Tantras popular with the Brahmins. These are Tripurānanda, Brahmānanda, Pūrṇānanda and Kṛṣṇānanda. The first three belong to Eastern Bengal and the last to Nadia. The Sarvavidyā family of Jessore too did much to popularise them in Central Bengal but at a later period than the others.

From all that has been said above it is apparent that in the twelfth century there were the following forms of religion in Bengal and in Eastern India.

(1) Brahminism. It was followed by 800 families of Rāḍhīya and Vārendra Brahmins and about a hundred families of other Brahmins, the descendants of many Kāyasthas who came from the west and those of the lower classes who served these families.

(2) Hīnayāna. This was followed on the west of the Ganges and especially in Tamluk.

(3) Mahāyāna. It was a religion of the higher-class Buddhist monks and higher-class Buddhist laity.

(4) Vajrayāna. This was the religion of the middle-class man and the married Buddhist clergy.

(5) Nāthism, which was professed by the Yogis who had numerous followers amongst the Buddhists and a few among the Brahminists.

(6) The Sahajiyā cult. It had numerous followers below the middle-class Buddhists and some among the lower class Brahminists.

(7) Tantrism. It had its followers among all classes, but among the higher-classes it was a subsidiary form of worship, among the lower it was the chief form.

(8) The Kālachakrayāna. It was purely Buddhist and more a religion of fear than of love or faith and was followed by the lowest classes.

In the closing years of the 12th century, India was overrun by the Muhammadans. They destroyed the Buddhist monasteries of note, appropriated the monastic lands for the use of soldiers and massacred monks by thousands, and burnt libraries wherever found. Mahāyāna was practically stamped out from Bengal. It lingered however in nooks and corners for two centuries more and was then lost altogether. Brahmins who lived on the lands granted to them by the Pālas, the Senas, and other kings lost their lands by the Muhammadan invasion; and they also lost the chief source of their income from Government service. They were compelled from this time to extend the sphere of their activity as priests and teachers.

The Muhammadans called the Indians, Brahminists and Buddhists alike, Hindus or Indians. The Brahmins were not slow to take advantage of this and to make it appear that the Buddhists did not exist. All the intellectual followers of Buddhism were either massaccred or compelled to fly away from the country. The Brahmins found themselves masters of the situation in the Indian or the Hindu community. Muhammadans either by force or by persuation converted a large number of the Buddhists into Islam. The vast number of Buddhist were like so many lambs without a shephard. The Vajrayānists, the Sahajiyās, the Nāthists and the Kālachakrayānists for a time maintained a separate existence, but many of their followers were either converted to Islam or forced to join the Brahmins. But the exclusive spirit of the Brahmins made the admission of only such people into their fold possible as would consent to be their out and out followers. They took these within the pale of their society and called them Navaçākha or the new branch. Those who tried to maintain a separate existence were excluded from the pale of their society and these formed the Anācharaṇīya Jāti or the depresssed classes.

It has been already stated that the Kaivarttas were expressly excluded from the pale of Buddhism except those that renounced their profession of the slaughter of animals. But the Kaivarttas were a powerful race. The Ancients called them Dasyus *i.e.*, powerful foreigners who troubled by their raids the inhabitants of the Aryan lands. In the eleventh century the Kaivarttas formed a powerful confederacy in the North Bengal under the leadership of Bhīma, expelled the Pālas from their capital Gauḍa, where they occupied a suburb and temporarily became rulers of Bengal. The Pālas considered the rising of the Kaivarttas as a revolt. After a long struggle they suppressed the revolt with a strong hand, yet the Kaivarttas were a power to be counted with. With their aid Ballāla conquered Northern Bengal, and tried his best to make a clean caste of them, and divided them by sending the more turbulent ones to defend the Southern frontier Dakṣiṇaghāṭa. Their leader was Maheca whom he made a Maṇḍalevara from which fact the Dakhiṇaghāta is still known as the Maṇḍalaghāṭa.

Those of the Kaivarttas who lived by fishing were not Buddhists, but those who took to the profession of agriculture and to the profession of arms were Buddhists and became to a great extent civilised and educated. They patronised men of letters equally with the Pālas. A medical work composed under the patronage of Bhīma is still extant. Their priests, the descendants of the Buddhist married clergy, still form a community by itself. At the present moment they call themselves Brahmins, because none but the Brahmins are recognised in the Hindu society as priests. The Kaivarttas forgetful of their past and forgetful of their old tradition are now attempting to call themselves Māhiṣyas and thereby raise themselves to the position of Vaiçyas, though degraded in status. One who knows the past history of India cannot forbear a smile at this.

What is true of the Kaivarttas is true of other degraded classes. The Yogis are now trying to take the holy thread and become Brahmins. They do not know what they were. They were real Yogis, being descendants of the Nāthas, that influencial class to which belonged Matsyendranātha, Gorakṣanātha, Mīnanātha, Āyinātha, Chauraṅginātha, and others. Their ancesters had numerous followers. Princes and potentates bowed before them. Many Nāthas are still worshipped in temples and holy places in Nepal and in Tibet. Gorakṣanātha is still wor-

-shipped as the principal deity by the Gorkha as a race. His temple at the Gorkha hill is still the resort of thousands of pilgrims. His temple opposite to that of Paçupatinātha is kept clean with scrupulous care. He has many temples in the plains of India. The Nāthas do not seem to have observed any distinction among the several classes when taking in followers. It appears that their faith was accepted as a subsidiary faith, subsidiary more to the Buddhists, than to the Brahminists.

The Dharmaghariā Yogis are to be found in large numbers in South-Western Bengal. The so-called Brahmins who beg with the image of Çītalā in their hands and come from Howrah and Midnapore districts are all Dharmaghariā Yogis. They do not put on the holy thread, but they use copper in some form or other on their person after their initiation to religious life. They worship Dharma at Dharma temples. From the locality they come, they seem most likely to be the survivals of the Hīnayānist monks of the Tāmralipta country. One of their community with his followers went to the Pagan in the thirteenth century and reformed Buddhism there (see Kalyani inscriptions). These are Buddhists to all intents and purposes. Dharma is more widely worshipped in this part of Bengal than in others. Many of these Dharma temples are maintained by lands which were granted to them many centuries ago.

Guptas.—Tatakara, Subhā-kara, and Prabhākara have already been mentioned. They composed works on the Buddhist rituals of the Mantrayāna school, and so they must have been learned Buddhists in the 9th century. Sādhu Gupta was a Sthavira of some note at Nālanda. He got a copy of Aṣṭasāhasrikā made at his expense and presented it to a Buddhist monastery at Baṭagrāma. There is evidence to show that many Guptas were Buddhists. Dipaŋkara, the writer of Açvavaidyaka, was a Buddhist and belonged to a wellknown Buddhist family. The Karas are not much respected among the present Vaidya class. The men of this caste studied Sanskrit in those of its branches which are enumerated in the commentary of Rāmachandra Kavi Bhāratī's Bhakticataka. They belonged originally to Bengal and Eastern India. They seemed to be the survival of the lay, learned and married Buddhist priests or Āryas. They never cared for the holy thread. Their claims to the Vaiçyablood dates from the middle of the 18th century and at the present moment they are advancing claims to the Brahminic rank. This may be justified in the sense that some of them were priests and still there is a large number of the Vāmāchāri Tantriks among them. Some of them became followers of Chaitanya and have adopted the calling of Gosvāmins or religious preceptors. The Vaidya community may not perhaps like the idea that they were at one time Buddhists. But they cannot explain their origin. They say they are a mixed caste formed by the cross-breeding of Brahmins and Vaiçyas. But their genealogies tell a different tale. They are descended from the fifty-one Vījapuruṣas who cannot be placed before the eleventh century. Their title Kavirāja shows that they knew Sanskrit, and they were superior Kavis by which term medical men in Bengal used to be designated.

How Buddhism fared under Brahminic sway is best evidenced by a study of the Buddhist community in Nepal. To the Brahmin the Buddhists are Anācharaṇīya. The King acting under the advice of the Brahmins may make some particular families or classes clean castes, but the bulk of them are outside the pale of Brahminic society. The descendants of the married clergy who still occupied Vihāras meant for monks and who cannot find sufficient work as priests, take to such arts and callings as would bring respectable wages without hard manual labour. Thus in Nepal, Goldsmiths, Carpenters and Painters all belong to the descendants of the married clergy. By an analogy of Nepal one can easily detect why Chhutārs and Sekrās have become Anācharaṇīya in Bengal. Formerly these two castes formed a part of the Buddhist community in Bengal and so the Brahmins have excluded them from the community. It is a curious feature in the Brahminic community that however unfavourable they may be to the Anācharaṇīya castes they are still more unfavourable to their priests now miscalled Brahmins. In Nepal too the Buddhist priests are subject to a greater share of the Brahmin's ire than their lay followers.

The merchant community in Nepal noted for their personal beauty, all belong to Buddhism and are for this reason excluded from the Brahminic society. For the same reason the merchant community in Bengal who stood by their Buddhist priests have been excluded and made Anācharaṇīya, while those who changed their priests have been taken within the Brahminic fold and made clean castes. But a study of the clean and unclean merchant community will show that both were originally Buddhists.

The Kāyasthas, if we exclude the descendants of those who are recognised as Kulīnas among the Dakṣiṇa Rāḍhīya and Vaŋgaja communities, and who were Brāhminic in their tendencies were mostly Buddhists. These are all Maulikas, *i. e.* they originally belonged to this country, a Buddhist country. In Dharmapāla's time there was a Vriddha Kāyastha who wrote Buddhist books and so late as 1436 A. D. the Kāyastha zamindars of Benugrāma in Sohinchari parganā were Buddhist. They had Buddhist Bhikṣus with them and they studied Buddhist books.

But below the Anācharaṇīya there are several castes still in Bengal, who do not even pretend to have the so-called Brahmin priests. They raise one of their caste-men to the priesthood and give him the title of Pandit. We read in the Vratamālāvadāna of the Buddhist that there were three classes of priests, Paṇḍitas, Çramaṇas and Brāhmaṇas. Tho position of the Paṇḍitas who are placed first in *the compound* is more honourable than that of either Çramaṇas or Brāhmaṇas. From the facts given above, which can be indefinitely multiplied, it would appear that in ancient Bengal before the Muhammadan conquest, the descendants of the five Brahmins and the five Kāyasthas were the only Brahminists. They had either induced or compelled others to come into their society. The rest of the community were Buddhists.

The case of the Sonār-Vaniās is decidedly a good one. They were Buddhists. Their leader in Bengal in the 12th century was Vallabha Āḍhya who had two forts Saŋghyakoṭi and Chandramāyuta. He was enormously rich, being the richest banker in Bengal. He married his daughter to a king of Magadha and the kings of Magadha were notoriously Buddhists. In the first part of his reign Ballāla was a Buddhist. It is said that he kidnapped the daughter of a Chaṇḍāla off on immoral purposes in order to attain Siddhi or success in life. The worshippers of Tārā, the Çakti of the Buddhists, think that long life may be attained by repeating hymns to that goddess after sitting on a Chaṇḍāla woman. This shows that in the beginning of his reign Ballāla though not a Buddhist directly had a strong tendency towards Tantric Buddhism ; but later on Siṁhagiri a Çaiva ascetic from the Joṣi-Maṭha in Garhwal became his Guru and under his advice Ballāla became a Çaiva and a patron of the Brahmins. As long as Ballāla showed Buddhistic tendencies Vallabha lent him money which enabled him to conquer the five Bengals. But in his later life after becoming Çaiva Ballāla wanted money for a war against Magadha, Vallabha refused to advance money. This led to a quarrel and Ballāla drove the Baniās away. They settled in the adjoining kingdoms of Tippera, Orissa, Behar and others. Those who remained in Bengal were degraded. Brahmins were prohibited from teaching them and officiating in their religious ceremonies. Thus the only chance for the Sonār-Baniās to be admitted into the Brahminist society was lost. The Vaidika Brahmins from the South sympathised with the Baniās and they incurred the displeasure of Ballāla and were not admitted to Kulīnism.

It is a well known fact that Buddhism does not make any distinction of caste in India. But in Nepal in the present day there is a sort of distinction between the priestly and the non-priestly occupations, and the different occupation of the laity. The distinction however is not so pronounced as in the Brahminic society. In the remote days, when Bengal was a Buddhist country, a distinction was observed among the several classes of the Buddhists. The unmarried monks were regarded with the greatest reverence, and the married clergy was regarded as the highest of castes. Next to them were the ruling and the merchant community. But there was a large class of labourers who belonged to the lowest occupations :—sweepers and others who enjoyed very little of the advantages of the social life. To these were denied the services of the barbars and sometimes of washermen. The necessities of the times sometimes made it imperative to ex-communicate persons, families and seven clans of a locality. These swelled the ranks of the lowest community.

After the Muhammadan conquest Brahminic ideals were super-imposed on the Buddhist ideals of society. The distinctions among the classes became more and more prominent till they developed into a regular caste-system. People forgot their old history, the history of their own distinction and began to think with the Brahmins that all distinctions were due either to cross breeding or to ex-communication. Thus a social edifice was built up in Bengal with the Brahmins forming the top-most part. The existence of Buddhism was forgotten. Masses of the Anācharaṇīya classes are the survivals of the forgotten Buddhism. These classes are depressed only in the eyes of the Brahmins and those who have come under the Brahminic influence. The more one would study the social history of Bengal, the more will one be convinced that the classes are not really depressed. They continue to be what they were, only they have lost their consciousness of a great past, intellectually, morally and socially. It was people of these classes that carried Buddhist ideals to Tibet and China, held commercial relations with the countries of Eastern and Southern Asia and were great in trade and in industry. We hear of long sea-voyages made even in the fifteenth century by the Bengal Bāniās, glowing descriptions of which are to be found in works of Manasār Bhāsān written by various poets of Bengal. With the advance of research the so-called depressed classes will regain the lost consciousness of their former glory. It is therefore necessary that Brahmins should take steps to conciliate them, and take them into their confidence.

Before the Muhammadan conquest, Bengal was divided between the two communities of Brahminists, and Buddhists, and after that the entire population was divided into the two great classes of Hindus and Muhammadans. The word Hindu literally means Indian, and is therefore capable of a very wide significance. The depressed classes are now as good Hindus as the Brahminists, though they have no common faith and common social organisation. If they are organised as a homogeneous community with common interests and common aspirations and receive the common appellation of Hindus, why should the *Mahomedans*, the domiciled Mahomedans, the *Christians*, and the domiciled Christians not be called Hindus as well, because they too have been living in India for many centuries and have the same interests and aspirations. If the depressed classes regain their consciousness and position in the Hindu society, the Hindu society will in near future include all the inhabitants of Bengal and thus the term will regain its radical and real significance.

Ask a Nepalese Buddhist how many religions are there in the world, and he will answer "there are two religions Gubhāju and Devabhāju" *i.e.*, the worship of the Gurus and the Devas. The Buddhists are Gubhāju for they worship their great Guru Buddha and the Brahmins are Devabhāju for they worship Devas. Buddhism and Hinduism have influenced each other greatly and now pure Gubhājus and Devabhājus are rare. When a Brahmin in the morning repeats his Vedic Sandhyā, he is a Devabhāju, but when he performs his Tantric Sandhyā or when he looks upon his Guru as the living embodiment of his God on earth he is a Gubhāju. The key-note of the distinction between Brahminism and Buddhism is the worship of God and the worship of Guru. But is there any one in Bengal who does not worship both. Even the unitarian Brāhma is no exception when he prays to one God, he is a Devabhāju, but when he observes the birthday of Rāmmohan Rāya and of Kesava Chandra he is a Gubhāju.

Now the distinction between the ancient Buddhists, and ancient Brahmins being this, it is possible to say what *amount of Buddhism and Brahminism* there is in the doctrine of any particular sect now flourishing in Bengal. As I have shown above all people are to some extent Devabhāju and to some extent Gubhāju. Intellectual people seem to be more Devabhāju than Gubhāju, but the less intellectual people are more Gubhāju than Devabhāju. The followers of Chaitanya making a pilgrimage to Nadia on the full-moon of Phālguna and keeping a complete record of the birth and death of the great preachers of their faith, are more Gubhājus than Devabhājus, they are more influenced by Buddhism than by Brahminism. The Karttābhajās to whom the Guru is the only Truth and every thing else illusion are most prominently Gubhāju ; that is, Buddhist. That they do not use the word Buddha need not deter us from calling them Buddhists ;

for in later times Buddhists were not known as Buddhists but as the followers of Guru contracted into 'Gu'. Do we not call the Buddhism in Tibet Lāmāism! But what does the word 'Lāma' mean? It simply means Guru. So the worship of Guru means direct or indirect influence of Buddhism and here is a criterion of the utmost importance. For an analysis of the doctrines of the various religious sects inhabiting Bengal and Eastern Iṇdia, and the consequent determination of the amount of Buddhism that have entered into them, the presence or absence of Buddha's name does not matter at all.

Under these circumstances the discovery of a new sect in Mayūrabhañja pre-eminently of the Gubhāju tendency and using some of the terms current in Mahāyāna Buddhism by Babu Nagendranāth Vasu is of the utmost importance to the social and religious history of the country. It shows how tenaciously the people still cling to their ancient faith though all memory of it seems to be lost. A trained eye can see through things, and Nagendra Babu seems to be eminently endowed with such a trained eye in matters relating to the social and religious history of this country.

For a long time, all thinking people of India wondered what became of Buddhism which had played so important a part in the history, life and literature of the country in olden times. Babu Akṣaya Kumāra Datta considered that the worship of Viṭhobā and Viṭṭhala was a survival of Buddhism. These deities are worshipped in the

Godāvari districts as the 9th incarnation of Viṣṇu. Jagannātha at Puri is still regarded as Buddha incarnate or Viṣṇu incarnate as Buddha.

It was, however, only about twenty years ago that researches in regard to the survival of Buddhism in Bengal began with some earnestness and I took some interest in the matter. These resulted in the discovery that the *pūjā* of Dharma Ṭhākur, so common in Western Bengal, is a survival of Buddhism. The discovery was held with delight in certain quarters and with strong opposition in others. But the researches continued and it was found that many of the Tantric cults came to Brahminism through Buddhism and the whole of the Tantric Literature was greatly influenced by it. The study of Buddhism in Nepal under Hindu supremacy showed that the Anācharaṇīya classes, at least some of them, were the remnants of the Buddhist population. Sahajiyās in Bengal had always been regarded as a recent development of Vaiṣṇavism, but the study of ancient manuscripts in Nepal showed that there were Sahajiyās also even in the Pāla period, and that they were strongly imbued with later Buddhist ideas. The Vaiṣṇava Sahajiyās are really a continuation of the old Buddhist Sahajiyās.

The Nāthas too were to a great extent a survival of Buddhism. It was subsequently found that life in Bengal, even the most orthodox Brahminic life, showed traces of Buddhist influence and Buddhist ideals. Balarāma Hāḍi who preached a new cult at Meherpur in Nadia at the beginning of the last century and died in 1857, and whose followers number by thousands in the adjoining districts, got his ideas from the still surviving Buddhism in the nooks and corners of Bengal. A few years ago, Mr. Gait placed in my hands some materials from which it was found that the Sarāki Tāntis who not only inhabit the Tributary Mahāls of Cuttack, but are to be found in the settled districts of Cuttack and Puri, still worship Buddha along with the Brahminic Gods in all their religious ceremonies and that the word Sarāki is simply a Prākrit form of the word Çrāvaka. The Sarākis are to be found in Bankura and Burdwan too. Although they bear a Buddhistic name, they seem to have forgotten all their Buddhism. The Cuttack Tributary Mahals were supposed to contain many relics of later Buddhism. The State of Baud named after Buddha was supposed to contain still a remnant of real Buddhist population. The researches of Babu Nagendra Nāth Vasu in the jungles of Mayūrabhañja have proved that these suppositions were not wrong. He has not only traced the existence of Buddhism from the time of the persecutions by Purusottama and his successor Pratāparudra, but discovered a new reformed faith, preached only during the last quarter of the 19th century. His book is exceedingly interesting and opens a new vista of research.

26, PATALDANGA STREET,
Calcutta, May 17th, 1911. — HARA PRASAD SHASTRI.

MODERN BUDDHISM

AND ITS

FOLLOWERS IN ORISSA.

CHAPTER I.

Rise of the different schools, from the 1st to the 15th Century.

Towards the end of the 1st Century of the Christian era, the Scythian King Kaniska held a council of Buddhists at Jālandhar. At this council the Buddhists were found to be divided into two schools, one following the purer doctrine of Buddha himself, in spite of all the difficulties and obstacles that he had placed in the way of attaining salvation ; this was named Hīnayāna or the Little Vehicle. The other,—while idealising Buddha with all his attributes,—introduced innumberable gods and demons, and added to the list of Buddhas and Bodhisattvas. This was styled the Mahāyāna or the Great Vehicle.

The Hīnayāna and the Mahāyāna schools of Philosophy then claimed Buddhism between themselves ; and these, again, were subdivided,—the former into Vaibhāsika and Sautrāntika, and the latter into Mādhyamika and Yogāchāra. The Mahāyāna school, however, had the predominant voice ; and the essence of its doctrine was "Sarvam Anityam, Sarvam Çunyam, Sarvam Anātman (All is transitory, all is void, all is non-ego.")*

Nāgārjuna, the founder and expounder of the Mādhyamika philosophy, flourished at the time of the Third Council. The end and aim of his philosophy was to bring about a compromise, as it were, between the Çramaṇas and the Brāhmaṇas, and to find out a midway where the adherents of these two, could meet and shake hands with one another. "Nāgārjuna both by examples and theory, taught that Brahmā, Viṣṇu, Çiva, Tārā and other deities possessed the attributes which Brāhmaṇas had assigned to them, and therefore were the proper objects of worship for help in worldly concerns. * * * * * Since his time the Brāhmaṇas began to regard the Mahāyāna Çramaṇas as their brother religionists."†

The doctrine of the Mahāçūnyam, as expounded by Nāgārjuna, as being the basis of the Mādhyamika philosophy, is to all intents and purposes but a reflection of the Great Brahma-Vāda, as inculcated in the Upaniṣads and the Gītā. And Dr. Kern is quite right when he observes that the Yogāchāras and the Mādhyamikas, the two true descendants of the Mahāyāna school, are but idealists in their own way. The former admits as reality nothing but

* D. T. Suzuki's *Mahayana Buddhism*, p. 44.
† Carat Chandra Dās's *Land of Snow*, p. 7.

Vijñāna, consciousness, and are in consequence, often designated Vijñāna-Vādins. But the Mādhyamikas are more sweeping in their pronouncements. They are absolute nihilists, carrying the theory of Name-and-Form to its extremes and denying all existence whatsoever, regarding the whole of the phenomenal world as a mere illusion. This nihilism of theirs may well be taken as the Buddhistic counterpart of the Scholastic Vedānta as taught by Çaŋkara.*

After Nāgārjuna, and second only to him, the chief expounder of the Mahāyāna philosophy was Vasubandhu. He was less wildly speculative than many of his predecessors and composed many commentaries, and was thus greatly successful in recasting, so to speak, the nihilism of the Mahāyāna school by giving it, as it were, an air of reality and tangibility. Thus Dr. Waddel says :—

"This intense mysticism of the Mahāyana led, about the fifth century, to the importation into Buddhism of the pantheistic idea of the soul (ātman) and Yoga or the ecstatic union of the individual with the Universal Spirit—a doctrine which had been introduced into Hinduism by Patañjali."†

The Yogāchāra School also, in its later development, received and assimilated some magic circles with mantras or spells about 700 A.D., and hence received the new appellation of Mantra-yāna.

---

* Dr. Kern's *Manual of Buddhism*, p. 127.
† Dr. L. A. Waddell's *Buddhism of Tibet*, p. 128.

But the Mahāyāna School did not stop there. Having once commenced the work of importation and assimilation, it went on with it, with all its zeal and vigour, and was before long almost a new thing. About the seventh century A.D. the development of the infatuating Tantrism, which practically verges on sorcery claiming a religious basis, attracted the notice of the Mahāyāna School, and ere long the idolatrous cult of 'female energies' was found grafted upon the theistic Mahāyāna and the Pantheistic mysticism of Yoga. And this Tāntrika phase of the Mahāyāna School reached its climax when it adopted, and assimilated with itself, the theory of the Kālachakra. Though laying no pretensions whatsoever to the consideration due to a philosophic system, this Kālachakra has an importance of its own as a doctrinal basis and deserves a passing notice here. It wants to establish a mysterious union between the terrible goddess Kālī of the Tāntrika system, and the Dhyānī Buddhas, nay, the Ādi-Buddha himself, of the Buddhistic system, and attempts to explain creation and the secret agencies of nature in the light of this union. In the tenth century, the Kālachakra system of the Mantrayāna School, as the result of further and further retrograde developments, passed into the system of the Vajrayāna or the thunderbolt-vehicle. This is the most depraved form, that the Buddhistic doctrine on its downward course of importation, assimilation and compromise, had ever assumed. According to this, the devotee may hope to attain the spiritual powers of siddhi—a stage admittedly far below Arhat-ship—with the joint aid of the supernatural Buddhas and the Ḍākas and the Ḍākinīs with their appropriate magic circles.*

As Dr. Kern rightly observes—"The doctrine of Buddhism in India from the eighth century downwards nearly coincides with the growing influence of Tantrism and Sorcery which stand to each other in the relation of theory to practice. The development of Tantrism is a feature that Buddhism and Hinduism in their later phases have in common."†

This is the history of Buddhism in India, as it rushed headlong towards superstition and decline. But a change, pregnant and comprehensive, was soon to pass over it, making it bright and glorious again. Towards the latter part of the eighth century, Dharma Pāla I of the Pāla Dynasty, was occupying the *masnad* of Gauḍa. He was a Buddhist, and grieved to find his religion sunk in superstition and grossness. He made up his mind to have its downward course arrested, and the faith purged of all the impurities and unwelcome elements. His spirit was projected, as it were, into the minds of his successors, and systematic and earnest endeavours were made by the successive wearers of the crown to restore Buddhism to its former height and grandeur. And considering the galaxy of good and pious souls flourishing at the time of Dharma Pāla II, Mahī Pāla I and Naya Pāla who

* Dr. Waddell's *Buddhism of Tibet*, p. 152.
† Kern's *Manual*, p. 133.

reigned from 1015 to 1060 A.D., we cannot but pronounce that their endeavours were largely crowned with success. The first and foremost amongst this group of great men was Dīpaṅkara Çrījñāna, otherwise known as Atiça. He was at the helm of the Vikramçila monastery from 1035 A.D. to 1038 A.D. Other notable names are Rāmāi Paṇḍit, Hāḍi Siddha, Kamalā Kuçila, Narendra Çrījñāna, and Dāna Rakṣita. Belonging to and professing the Tāntrika cult, they rose much above it and made themselves distinguished by their teachings and lives of piety, self-abnegation and self-renunciation. They were not, thus, to be ranked with the followers of the black Tantrism who made the enjoyment of material comforts their goal of life.

The irreligion and corruption which followed in the wake of the Tāntrika cult in its onward course, the latter taking the place of the spirit of its teachings and practices, permeated through and through the lives of both Hindus and Buddhists of the time, and deadened their spiritual sense. A tide of reaction, in the case of Buddhism, had already set in, as we have seen, with Dharma Pāla I, towards the end of the eighth century. And before the eleventh century had come to its close, divisions were effected in the camp of the Tāntrika Buddhism, owing to a revival of the religious spirit by some of the greatest thinkers and men of the time. The principal divisions were—the way of Pravṛtti, and the way of Nivṛtti. The goal of life which the Pravṛtti-mārgin (those who took to the path of Pravṛtti,) desired to set before them, was emancipation attainable only through enjoyment, life being indissolubly linked with weal and woe. And they proceeded to collect authoritative works in support of their view, to appeal to the hearts of the masses and win them over to their side.

The goal of the Nivṛtti-mārgin on the other hand was entire deliverance of the soul from the Pravṛtti. which is constantly at work—the source of all our pain and sufferings,—and the subsequent attainment of the blissful state, called Nivṛtti,—a complete annihilation or deadening of all the appetites and desires. Habitual abstraction of the mind from all pleasures and pains, will enable a man to know what Nivṛti is ; and Tapas and Dhyāna are set down as the means for the realization of this habitual abstraction. But the highest ideal that this class of Buddhists set before their mental eyes was the acquisition of the knowledge of the Great Unconditioned Void or Mahā-Çūnyam. It was the highest flight of the Mādhyamika philosophy, and the fountain-head of all ideals and inspirations to its followers. Once more, inspired and fired with zeal and enthusiasm, they set about to collect the cardinal doctrines of the Mādhyamika School, and set them forth again in a more attractive and popular form. Amongst this class we find such names as Aticā Dīpaŋkara, Narendra Çrījñāna and others.

As stated above, these two mārgas or ways were essentially different from one another, the former aiming at the realization of the unity of the Ādi-Buddha and Ādi-Prajnā (Puruṣa and Prakṛti) through the love and enjoyment of the world ; and the latter, at the absorption of the soul in the Great Çūnyam through purity, love and renunciation.

It was in Gauḍa that both these systems of theology and religion first germinated and developed. Only a few years ago Mahāmahopādhyāya Haraprasād Çāstri came across several ancient Bengali manuscripts in Nepal, dating from eight to nine hundred years back : and on examination these were found to belong to the Pravṛtti-Mārga School, recording the development of its thoughts and ideas in their several stages.

When Buddhisim had practically vanished from this country, the pernicious system propounded by the Pravṛtti Mārga lingered in the Sahajiā cult of the Vaiṣṇavas and did incalculable mischief to that society. The influence which these two schools of thought exercised upon the minds of all sections of the community was considerable. Advocating the fullest enjoyment of life the Pravṛtti Mārga system soon became a powerful instrument of vice in the hands of many inculcating the noxious practices of the Sahajiyā cult. The Nivṛttī-mārga system was a no less potent factor in moulding and regulating the thoughts of society, as is evidenced by a critical study of the Çūnya-Purāṇa and Dharma-Maŋgala literature and several other Oriya manuscripts, recently brought to light from some of the backward villages of Mayūrabhañja. Remnants of its former influence are still discernible in the manners and customs of the Bāthuri tribe and the Mahimā-dharmin sect of Mayūrabhañja.

What we aim at in this chapter is to discuss briefly the influence which the Nivṛitti-Mārga once exercised upon the minds of the country and the part it played in the history and growth of a comparative religion. The writings extant on the subject are, however, very frequently enveloped in a peculiar mysticism. They ascribe, for instance, to Çrijñana, Rāmāi Paṇḍit and the other sages of the time, we have referred to above, all sorts of miracles and supernatural feats. Whatever may be the value of these assertions, it is at any rate true that the goal of life they aimed at and taught others to aim at, was the attainment of *Bambha Nibbāna** which really refers to the Buddhistic idea of Salvation.

It may not be out of place to note in passing that the reputation and influence of Atiça extended over the whole of lower Bengal and from there up to Bhoṭa (Tibet). The fame of Rāmāi Paṇḍit spread over the whole of Rāḍha† and Hāḍi Siddha's name exercised for long a magic influence in the eastern provinces of Bengal.

---

* *Vide* Rāmāi Pandit's Cunyapurāna published by the Bangiya Sāhitya Parisad, 1909.

† Mayurabhanja, is situated close to Rārha. Nay, to the people of Orissa, Mayurabhanja itself is known as Rārha.

It has been proved beyond all shadow of a doubt by Mahāmahopādhyāya Haraprasād Çāstri, that the Dharma cult which even now counts amongst its followers a good many people of the lower classes of Bengal, was founded and inaugurated by Rāmāi Paṇḍit. We shall try to show later on that the result of the endeavours made by the Pāla Kings to improve the depraved religious tone of the country and more especially the personal influence of Rāmāi Paṇḍit in this direction, were not confined within the limits of Mayūrabhañja, but pervaded the whole of Orissa. M. M. Çāstri has clearly shown that the central force of Rāmāi Paṇḍit's works was the doctrine of the Mahā-Çūnyam or the Great Void, which is again the heart and soul of the Mādhyamika philosophy. The bright and sparkling description or Dhyāna of Dharma in which he indulges, is itself a strong and clear proof of this. Nowhere in the whole range of Buddhist scriptures do we come across, a more luminous passage than the one in which he describes the Çūnyam. And we cannot do better than quote a few lines from it :—

> "यस्यान्तीनादिमध्यो न च करचरणौ नास्तिकायो निर्नादं ।
>
> नाकारो नैव रूपं न च भयमरणे नास्ति जन्मनि यस्य ।
>
> योगीन्द्रैर्ज्ञानगम्यं सकलदलगतं सर्व्वलोकैकनाथं ।
>
> भक्तानां कामपूरं सुरनरवरन्दं चिन्तयेत् शून्यमूर्त्तिम् ।"

"He who has neither a beginning nor an end, nor a middle ; who has, further, neither hands nor feet, neither body nor voice ; neither form nor image ; and who is afraid neither of birth nor death:—He who is knowable only by the greatest of the Yogis, sages; who underlies and upholds all classes of men; who is the sole lord of all the worlds (*i.e.* the whole creation); who brings about the realizations of the desires of his devotees, and confers boons upon gods and men alike. Devoid of all forms and figures as the void itself, he is to be meditated upon."

We also find a similar passage in his Çūnya-Purāṇa :—

"शून्यरूपं निराकारं सहस्रविघ्ननाशनम् ।
सर्व्वपर: परो देव तस्मात्त्वं वरदो भव ॥"

"Thou art destitute of all forms and images, and art the destroyer of all perils and disasters; thou art above everything and the god of gods. Hence mayest thou be pleased to confer boons upon us."

Svayambhū-Purāṇa of Nepal is a Buddhistic work of wide renown and some merit. Amongst its prefatory Çlokas we find the following, the underlying idea of which is a distinct echo of that conveyed in the above quotations :—

"नमो बुद्धाय धर्म्माय सङ्घरूपाय वै नम: ।
स्वयम्भुवे वियच्छान्त (?) भानवे धर्म्मधातवे ॥
अस्ति नास्ति स्वरूपाय ज्ञानरूपस्वरूपिणे ।
शून्यरूपस्वरूपाय नामरूपाय वै नम: ॥"

"All obeisance to thee who art Buddha, Dharma, and Saŋgha personified and who art self-existent, and who art in Çūnya, the sun itself—all serene and sublime; and the essence of all religion. All obeisance to thee who art both existent and non-existent, and also omniscient; and whose form is Çūnya and who art but one and the same with the Name itself."

But of all the existing Buddhistic writings of the Mahāyāna School, by far the most important is Prajñā-pāramitā. This is to the Buddhists what Vedās are to the Brāhmaṇas. Prajñā-Pāramitā, as mentioned above, is a Sutra Çāstra of the Mahāyāna School, and is mainly devoted to an elaboration of the doctrine of Çūnyatā. In the chapter on Buddhistic Philosophy in his celebrated work of Sarvadarçana-Saṁgraha, the renowned Mādhavāchārya has dwelt at some length upon the theory of the Çūnya. The following is a quotation from it :—

"अस्ति नास्ति तदुभयानुभयचतुष्कोटिविनिर्मुक्तं शून्यरूपं" इत्यादि ।

"The ultimate principle, then, is a void emancipated from four alternatives—from reality from unreality, from both reality and unreality combined, and from neither reality nor unreality."*

But in spite of all this, Buddhism, otherwise known as Sad-Dharma, gradually lost its hold upon the minds of the cultured classes of Bengal as M. M. Haraprasād Çāstri has shown. In its deteriorated form it merely retained a

---

* *Sarva-Darcana-Samgraha*, translated by E. B. Cowell and A. E. Gough, p. 22—23.

lodgment in the minds of the superstitious priests of the Dharma and Çītalā cults and their numerous followers, and there it still lurks.

Dr. Kern also writes to this effect:—"After the invasion of the country by the Mahomedans in A. D. 1200, the monasteries of Odantapura and Vikrama-Çilā were destroyed, and the monks were killed or fled to other countries. The learned Çākya-çrī went to Orissa and afterwards to Tibet."

But Buddhism also found a hiding-place, as it were, in the Deccan, as we are told by the same author.—"Many emigrants from Magadha rejoined their brethren in the South and founded colleges on a modest scale, in Vijayanagara, Kaliŋga, and Koŋkaṇa."*

Dr. Kern is one of the best authorities on the history of Buddhism. The above quotations from his "Manual" establish it beyond doubt that after the Universities of Nālandā and Vikrama-çilā were destroyed, and the wave of Muhammadan conquest had swept past Magadha and Gauḍa, the surviving ministers of Buddhism migrated to Utkala and there built new monasteries. And these citadels, in the wildernesses of Orissa, not only acted as a bar to arrest the tide of extinction, but largely helped the growth and gradual expansion of the religion.

The zeal and enthusiasm of these emigrants did not end with the construction of monasteries. Right earnestly did they devote themselves to a study of both the ancient and modern

* *Manual of Buddhism*, p. 134.

scriptures of the faith, and fought hard and long against the tide of extinction that threatened to engulf them. Even when the Tibetan pilgrim, Buddha Gupta Tathāgata Nātha, visited Utkala towards the latter half of the 17th century, he found old chaityas, stūpas and various other relics of the faith which once had so strong a hold upon the minds of the people residing there. He also met some living priests of the Dharma Cult.

Under these circumstances, we fully hoped we should find sufficient materials to prove the enormous influence that this religion once exercised upon the minds of the people in Utkala. And indeed it affords us no little satisfaction to report that within a short time and without much trouble we came across very many evidences of the sway once exercised by the various sects of Buddhism in Mayūrabhañja. In the forest tracts adjacent to Baḍasāi and Kiching in Mayūrabhañja we have discovered several Oriya manuscripts shedding a flood of light upon the later phases of Buddhism. Both from what we are able to glean from these manuscripts, and as the result of our ethnological researches, we have come to the irresistible conclusion that the influence of the Dharma Cult and the later phases of Buddhism still lingers in the hearts, and regulates the lives, of the people of this place. Unconsciously, as if instinctively, they follow the manners and customs and observe the rites and ceremonies that gathered round the Mahāyāna School in the days of its decline.

CHAPTER II.

ETHNOGRAPHIC DISCOVERY.

The Buddhistic relics discovered in the village of Baḍasāi, owed their preservation from absolute destruction and oblivion entirely to the commendable zeal and care of the Bāthuri tribe. This tribe, which is known in Mayūrabhañja as Bāthuri, has, in Keonjhar and the remaining Gaḍjāt States, received two other appellations, *viz.*, Bāhuri or Bāuri.

Balarāma-dāsa, in his commentary on Gaṇeça-vibhūti, entitled Siddhānta-ḍambara, written in the 16th century, thus refers to the Bāthuri tribe :—

"निराकार दक्षिणरु विप्र होए जात ।
उत्तर अङ्गरु जान गोपाल सम्भूत ॥ १७
वदन अन्तरे बिश्वामित्र मुनि कहि ।
ताहांकु अङ्गरे वाउरि जात होइ ॥ १८ * * *
विश्वामित्र जेष्ठ सुत पुत्र हादे जान ।
सेइटि वाउरि अनन्तकाण्डी नाम ॥ २१
औरथाख्या दास इति आचार्य्य अच्छन्ति ।
वाजपेय दोवे इति दासे बोलावन्ति ॥ २२
पाणि मिश्र पति बोलि सात जाति जान ।
अत्र चैतनी छन्ति हेतु करि मान ॥ २३
वसिष्ठ अङ्गरु बाबु विप्रकुल एहि ।
सूत्र ए वलिया एहि नाम गुटी कहि ॥२४ * *

तार तहुँ तेर सुत हइल जनम।
ताहार पत्नीर नाम पद्मालया जान ॥ २५
कनिष्ठ पत्नीरे चित्र उर्व्वशी तार नाम।
गन्धकेशी वलिण तार दुतिय भार्य्या जान। २६
वायुरेखा वलिण से चतुर्थक कहि।
बार सुत जन्म हेले चारि पत्नी तंहि ॥ २८
नाम ताह्वाङ्कर एवे कहुअछि शुण।
संशय लागिल मोते कहिवा आपन ॥२९। * * * *।

एवे वाउरि बार पुत्र नाम कहिवा। पद्मालयापुत्र दुलि वाउरि अटन्ति ब्राह्मणसङ्गे वेद पढ़ुथान्ति। ब्राह्मण जेष्ठ वाउरि कनिष्ठ। ए पढ़ुथिले राजा प्रतापरुद्रङ्क ठारु गोप्य करि रखिअच्छन्ति। * * * * पद्मालया पुत्र वायोकाण्डी परमानन्द भोइ राधो शासमल। गीत—

उर्व्वशीर तिन पुत्र अठई प्रमाण।
कुशसर्व्वा वोलि तार जेष्ठ पुत्र नाम ॥
विधुकुश वोलि तार कनिष्ठ पुत्र कहि।
उर्व्वकुश वोलि तार तिन पुत्र कहि ॥
ए तिन वाउरि, काजा गन्ध ॥
केशिठारु तिन सुत हादे जान ॥
एके एके कहिदेवा ताह्वाङ्कर नाम।
जेष्ठपुत्र प्रयशा वलिण नाम कहि।
उद्यम प्रतिवलिटी कनिष्ठ पुत्र कहि ॥
साधुप्रम वलि तिन सुतर जे नाम।
वाद्युति वलिण नाम अति अनुपाम ॥
वायुरेखा तिन सुत नाम देवा कहि।
जयसर्व्वा वोलि जेष्ठ सुतटी अटइ ॥
इन्दुसर्वा वोलि नाम कनिष्ठ नन्दन।
महावीर्य्यकेतु वोलि एहि ठारु शुण ॥
ए तिन नन्दन जे शवर अटन्ति।
सत्य कहुअछि शुण उमार सन्तति ॥
बार जाति वाउरि जे एहि प्रतिरोध।
भिन्न भिन्न करि एहा जाति गोत्र शोध ॥

दुलि वाउरि, काह्नाल, अजय काह्नाल, गुरु काह्नारि, ऐरि, वाउरि, शवर, जुयाङ्ग, जादु, भादु, गुरु, नुधन। * * गीत—

गणेश वोइले प्रभु मोते आज्ञा हउ।
ए चारि दुहिता जात होले काँहि॥
पद्मालया जाहा नाम अमूल्यटी सेहि।
निराकार दक्षिण अङ्गरु जात होइ॥
द्वितिय भार्य्या चित्र उर्व्वशी ता नाम।
गन्धकेशी वोलिण ताहार दासी जान॥
वायुरेखा अटइ गन्धकेशी दासी।
ए तिन हे पद्मालया दासी जे अटन्ति॥
एवे कहिथिलु वेणी पाठक लक्षण।
सावधान होइ शुण उमार नन्दन॥
पद्मालया तिन पुत्र जेष्ठ से प्रमाण।
विष्णुङ्क सङ्गते से हुयन्ति सम्भाषण॥
शङ्खासुर मारि प्रभु शङ्ख ताङ्कु दिले।
पञ्चजन शङ्ख तुम्भ सम्भाल वोइले॥
आउ नव भाइ अम्भ कुइ न जुगाइ।
विचारि जानिलेटी संशय केला सेहि॥" (१२ स अध्याय)

Whatever may otherwise be the value of these lines, they possess at least some historical interest. From them we obtain glimpses into the origin of the Bāthuris or Bāuris. Similar stories about origins are also to be met with in the Purāṇas,—but the story of Siddhānta-ḍambara is not corroborated by any Paurāṇika work, whether Hindu or Buddhistic. In all probability it is either a traditional history of the tribe, passing for generations from mouth to mouth, and given a tangible literary shape by the poet,—or based upon materials drawn from some other work existing at the time, but now either buried in oblivion or quite extinct.

2

The author has traced this tribe back to the fountain-head of all vitality and creation. He says :—From the right side of the Nirākāra sprang the Vipras into existence and from his mouth Viçvāmitra ; and from this Viçvāmitra the Bāuris came into being. The Vipras were, in their turn, divided into seven classes, *e.g.*, Çrī, Ratha, Dāsa, Miçra, Āchārya, Pāni and Pati. All these are mentioned as sons of Vaçiṣṭha. From the right side of the Nirākāra also sprang, in full bloom, the goddess Padmālayā, who was married to Viçvāmitra. The fruit of this union was a son, named Ananta-kāṇḍi Bāuri, and afterwards Duli Bāuri. It is also said that Duli Bāuri and his descendants studied the Vedas with the Brāhmaṇas, who were regarded as their elder brothers. Bāyokāṇḍi, Paramānanda Bhoi, and Rādhosāsmala—the three descendants of Padmālayā—are the Duli Bāuris. Chitrorvaçi was the second wife of Viçvāmitra, by whom he had three sons, *viz.*, Kuçasarvā, Vidhukuça and Urbakuça, from whom the Bāuris are descended. Viçvāmitra married another wife, *viz.* Gandhakeçī, who, too, blessed him with three sons—Prayaçā, Udyama and Sādhudharma ; and these came to be known as Bāghutis. Viçvāmitra had yet another consort in Vāyurekhā, who also was the mother of the same number of sons. They were named Jayasarvā, Vijaya-sarvā and Vijāya-ketu, and founded the Çavara tribe. These four castes, *viz.*, Duli Bāuri, Bāuri, Bāghuti and Çavara, came afterwards to be divided into twelve sub-castes. Although no Hindu or Buddhistic scripture is available to support the theory of the origin of the Çavara, in its entirety, yet it may be recorded here that in the Aitareya Brāhmaṇa of the Ṛgveda, the Çavaras are described as descendants of the sage Viçvāmitra. Hence we are of opinion that the description of Siddhānta-ḍambara is not entirely wanting in historical importance.

While describing the origin of the Bāuris, the author of Sidhānta-ḍambara has incidentally touched upon a very important fact. He says :— Of the three sons of Padmālayā, the eldest had once a friendly meeting with Viṣṇu, who killed Saŋkhāsura and gave him the Saŋkha. In a similar way five of the descendants of the same goddess by these sons received various friendly favours from Viṣṇu, while the nine remaining sons of Viçvāmitra by his three other wives had not been favoured even with the privilege of touching Viṣṇu's person.

We scarcely think it would be very wide of the mark to infer from this that the word Saŋkha here means nothing but a Buddhistic Saŋgha. In this interpretation of Saŋkha as Saŋgha, we are supported by the Çūnya-Purāṇa, in which Saŋkha is very frequently used for Saŋgha. The common people in their ignorance of the teachings of Buddhism and its terminology, either misspelt Saŋgha as Saŋkha, or mistook Saŋkha for Saŋgha which really means a congregation of Buddhistic monks. The only probable interpretation of Viṣṇu's killing Saŋkhāsura and giving the Saŋkha to Padmālayā's son is that the eldest member of the Bāuri community became a Saŋghādhipa, *i.e.*, chief of a Buddhistic fraternity, after destroying the enemies of the Saŋgha. Thus, we believe, it was that the sons of Padmālayā and their descendants obtained admittance to the fold of the Buddhistic Saŋgha, while the remaining sons of Viçvāmitra by his other wives, with their descendants, were thrown into the shade, and occupied an inferior position in society, merely because they could obtain no such admittance, or, in other words, had not themselves converted to Buddhism.

The author of Siddhānta-ḍambara makes this clear in the following lines:—

"पद्मालयापुत्र दुलि बाउरि अटन्ति ब्राह्मण सङ्गे वेद पढ़ुथान्ति । ब्राह्मण जेष्ठ बाउरि कनिष्ठ । ए पढ़ुखिले राजा प्रतापरुद्रङ्क ठारु गोप्य करि रखिअच्छन्ति ।"

"Duli Bāuri was Padmālayā's descendant; he would read the Vedas with the Brāhmaṇas. The Brāhmaṇa was older than he. The fact of the Bāuri studying the Vedas was kept concealed from King Pratāparudra."

Hence it is evident that the Bāuris were regarded as equal in rank with the Brāhmaṇas and that they observed the rites and followed the observances of Buddhism until the time of King Pratāparudra Deva of Orissa.

We learn from Mr. Sterling's *Orissa* that although the followers of Buddhism were at first received with form and treated with marked consideration by Pratāparudra Deva, they were afterwards persecuted by his court. Now, reading the history of Utkala together with that of Siddhānta-ḍambara, one must accept, as the only natural conclusion, our belief that it was the dread of persecution by the king that compelled the Buddhist priests of the Bāuri caste to seek shelter in concealment. And to evade these persecutions and avoid incurring the displeasure and disfavour of the Brāhmaṇas, they played the hypocrite by adopting the religious observances and practices of the latter. Further, in order completely to hoodwink these vigilant dragons of the Brāhmanic faith they substituted the names of Hindu gods and goddesses for those of their own. Notwithstanding all this apparent hypocrisy, however, they sincerely believed that Buddha was in reality an *avatára* of Viṣṇu, and as such they felt justified in substituting the name of Viṣṇu for his.—Even then, Çūnyavāda was the highest goal of their religious aspirations, and they consigned Brahmā, Viṣṇu and Çiva—their adopted gods—to inferior positions. But placed, as they were, under ban and anathema bv the king and the leaders of society, their social status was no higher than that of the Ḍomas and the Ḍoma Paṇḍits of Bengal who professed the Dharma cult.

We find the following lines in Siddhānta-ḍambara :—

"कलियुगे न कुइव। वाउरि कुइले सकल पातक चय हेव
वोलि विष्णुमाया करि गोप्य कोरि रखि अच्छन्ति ।
शुन हे गणेश वड़ गहनए गुप्त करि थुइवु ।
एथि सकाशरु बाउरि गार काटिले ब्राह्मण निभाइ पारन्ति नहि।
मूर्ख पातक च्चय हेव वोलि भ्राप्यकु भानियान्ति ।" (१२ अः)

"They are not to be touched in the Kaliyuga. But a touch of their bodies will extirpate all the sins. Hence Viṣṇu, through his māyā, has kept them in concealment."

Here, in the same breath, the author both decries and extols the Bāuris. Probably to complete their disguise and help them to conceal themselves, he says the Bāuris are unworthy of being touched. Yet in the next line he speaks of them in such high terms as can fall only from the lips of one who has himself been either a staunch believer in Buddhism or a Bāuri Paṇḍit like so many Ḍoma Paṇḍits of Bengal. The positions of these two classes of Paṇḍits were almost identical, although differing widely in their religious systems. Dharma occupied the highest place in the pantheon of the Ḍoma Paṇḍits; while, as we learn from Siddhānta-ḍambara, the Bāuris, not unlike the Mahāyānists of yore, held Mahāçūnyatā or Çūnya-Brahman as the sole cause of the entire universe. We obtain sufficient glimpses of the Çūnyavāda from the writings of the votaries of the different sects and sub-sects that sprang from latter-day Buddhism.

We have seen before that in the 16th century, up to the time of Rājā Pratāparudra of Utkala, Buddhism was the prevailing creed of Orissa. Although, owing to persecutions at the hands of the king, its influence began subsequently to wane, Buddhism was never wholly extirpated from the province. The crusade carried on against its followers, no doubt, compelled them to take refuge in the impregnable hilly parts of the country. Speaking of Mukunda Deva, the last independent King of Orissa, whose dominions extended from Triveṇī in the North to Ganjam in the South, *Pagsam Jon-Zan*, a Tibetan work written by Sampo Khampa, states that this King favoured Buddhism, and Buddhists were found in large numbers residing in his territories. We quote from it the following :—

"Mukunda Deva (Dharma-Rāja) King of Otivisa (Orissa) who favoured Buddhism, became powerful. His power extended up to Magadha. He, too, did some service to the cause of Buddhism."

In Siddhānta-ḍambara the Bāuri is mentioned as one of the nine classes of Brāhmaṇas, although, it is added, he was, in the time of the author, regarded as 'unworthy of being touched.' Now the question is whether, as stated by the author of Siddhānta-ḍambara, the present Bāthuris are in any way connected with the Brāhmaṇas. To this, from the various materials that we were able to glean in the course of our ethnological survey in Mayūrabhañja, we are in a position to reply that the Bāthuri tribe does really belong to the Aryan race. Ample proofs of this are scattered all over the country. To select at random from amongst a long list of such proofs, the fine specimens of architecture in the impregnable Simlipāla hills of Mayūrabhañja, the ancient stone temple named Āthāradeula, and similar other buildings, and the great stone fort of Joshipur or Daspur are unmistakable indications of their past culture and civilization, and go far in establishing their Aryan connection. It was only a few years back that this people were said to occupy the exalted positions of rulers, ministers and commanders. Bāthuris themselves believe that the Aryan blood runs in their veins; and are strongly convinced that they are in all respects on a par with the Brāhmaṇas. Even now they are found wearing the sacred thread; and like the Brāhmins they observe the 'ten days' mourning' and perform the *çrādh* ceremony on the eleventh day. On the day of the *çrādh*, Brāhmaṇas and Vaiṣṇavas dine in the house of the performer of the ceremony. The greatest personage of this tribe is now-a-days honoured with the title of Mahāpātra. On the occasion of the marriage of a son or a daughter, the Bāthuri house-holder has to give away a piece of cloth, ten betel-nuts and one hundred betels, as marks of honour to the Mahāpātra. And so great is the honour that he enjoys among his own people that on every festive occasion his approval has first of all to be sought and obtained. The Mahāpātra family of Mayūrabhañja proper is believed to have descended from the eldest branch and those of Ādipur and Dasapur from the youngest. Although occupying an inferior position in society, they themselves jealously regard their tribal self-respect and family prestige. No true Bāthuri will ever be induced to partake of the food cooked even by a Brāhmaṇa. If ever any member of their society in any way violates their social rules or is found to have illicit connection with any woman of any other caste, he suffers the extreme penalty of excommunication. They offer their religious homage to Dharmarāja, Jagannātha* (Baḍam), Kinchakeçvarī and Bāuri Thākurāṇī.

No writer has yet fully dwelt upon the ethnology of this ancient people. We therefore propose giving here rather a detailed account of their manners and customs. As has already been observed the Mahāpātras are the foremost in rank among the Bāthuris. Their ancestors were the rulers of Simlipāla, where remnants of their past glory may still be seen. Of these we have already spoken. Branches of this line are now living in Bāmuria, Joshipur or Dasapur and Ādipurgarh. From Māhapātra Sacchidānanda Dāsa of Ādipurgarh we have learnt that his ancestor of the fourteenth remove with his two brothers left his ancestral home at Jamunākula among the hills of Simlipāla, owing to the ravages of tigers. The eldest, who was the ruler of the state of Simlipāla removed to Bāmuria near Khuṇṭā Karkachia in Bhañjabhūma. The second and the third (youngest) migrated respectively to Ādipurgarh and Daspurgarh. Their descendants are still living in those places.

Another branch of the Bāthuri zamindars is to be found at Karañjiāgarh. This family is related to the Mahāpātras spoken of above, though sprung from a different stock.

* To the Buddhists of Nepal Dharmarāja and Jagannātha are only other names of Buddha.

We have heard both from Mahāpātra Sacchidānanda and his Vyavahartā (counsellor) Ananta Dāsa the following story of creation :—

Çūnya Mahāprabhu alone existed before creation. From Him sprang Vedamātā, of whom were born the fifty-six crores of beings and the world. They added that this account of the creation was to be found in numerous manuscripts of Simlipāla. Of these they themselves once possessed a large number, all of which had, however, been destroyed by fire. They also furnished us with an account of the origin of their own tribe. The following is the gist of what they said. In the beginning there was nothing but Çūnya; and from the arm (bāhu) of Çūnya Mahāprabhu sprang into existence the founder of their tribe. And it was for this (*i.e.*, their origin from the bāhu or arm of the creator) that the tribe came to be known as Bāhuri or Bāthuri. In course of time this tribe began to branch off into a large number of *Khilis*, *i.e.*, families, such as :—

Kuçamāliā,	Pāṭaliyā,
Biçāla,	Pātra,
Purihāra,	Kumār (Kuŋar),
Moḍei,	Khanḍei,
Dāsa,	Khālpāriyā,
Giri,	Çaŋkhiyāl,
Kapuṇḍia,	Māṇika,
Dhala,	Kānachikaniyā,
Çūliya,	Māṭiyān,
Simaḍaŋkiyā,	Jariyāl,
Senāpati,	Maigaḍabiçāla,

Khāṭuā,	Jāmuṇḍiā,
Rānāsiyā,	Danāyik,
Jhariāl,	Rupjitmarāī,
Rāmagaḍia,	Mṛḍiyā,
Bāgjaḍiā,	Bāragāñiyā,
Paniyāḍiyā,	Gāmbhāriyā,
Bārsāliyā,	Kalpāḍiyā,
Mushāpāliyā,	Kolāpāḍiyā,
Taṇḍakhāliyābiçāla,	Rāi-ṭhāñiyā,
Rāut,	Nimbāl,
Bāgchampiyāpātra,	Pichhaliyā,
Sundarghariāpātra,	Khejarpāṭiyā.

Each khili is regarded as one integral family, no nuptial alliance being allowed between members of one and the same khili. But such an alliance between members of different khilis is not prohibited. On the contrary they are very liberal on this point. One may even marry the daughter of his mother's own brother. Each of the khilis has again its gradations of rank, consisting of four orders, *viz.*, 1, Mahāpātras, 2, Nāyakas; 3, Pāiks; and 4, Muliyās, or the labouring class. They have four *gotras*, *viz.*, Parāçara, Nāgaça, Kāçyapa, and Pārdhyā. Kuçamāliyas and Biçālas occupy the foremost rank among the khilis; Khālpāriyas and the rest are all below them. Kuçamāliyas are reported to be descendants of Rāmapāla or Rāma Rājā of Simlipāla. From Siddhānta-ḍambara we learn that from the Formless sprang Viçvāmitra from whom there descended Kuçasarbā, Bidhukuça, and Aurbakuça. These latter are looked up to as having been the three Kuças or the earliest known progenitors of the Bāthuri tribe. The Kuçamāliyās of Bāmuriyā, Ādipur and Daspur also claim descents from Kuça.

Let us next turn our attention to the customs of the Bāthuris. Various ceremonies are gone through to solemnise the nativity of their children. Just on the seventh day after birth the body of the babe is besmeared with an unguent consisting of ground turmeric and mustard oil, and bathed in water: on the ninth day it is shaved, bathed and purified. Then on the twenty-first day the child is given a name (which corresponds to being "christened") and wrapped in a new piece of cloth. And on this day the family preceptor and Vaisṇavas are feasted, a horoscope of the child is cast by an astrologer, and worship is offered to Kalaça, Ganeça and the tutelary deities of the ten directions. In the tenth or eleventh month the Annaprāçana ceremony (when the child for the *first* time in its life takes rice and other solid food) is celebrated. Fresh cooking utensils and brand-new pieces of cloth are distributed and friends and relatives feasted on the occasion. Then several years are allowed to elapse, but when the boy comes to be seven or eight years old, he has to pass through a ceremony which is known as Karṇabedha, *i.e.*, the piercing of the ears. Again, on reaching the age of ten or eleven, his period of study commences, but does not continue long. The marriage ceremony is generally celebrated in the twelfth or the fourteenth year, the ceremony of *Upanayana* or conferring the sacred thread, taking place immediately before wedlock.

Girls are generally bestowed in marriage between the tenth and the twelfth year, though cases are not rare when they are married a littie earlier or later. When both the parties close with the terms of marriage, they enter into what may be called an agreement, a lekhāpatra, equally binding upon both of them, to the effect—that if either of them fails or declines to give his son or daughter in marriage on the day appointed, the bond is forfeited to the other and the defaulter becomes liable to the payment of a certain fine, also specified in the contract as penalty. After this, and in order solemnly to ratify the terms of the agreement, a peculiar ceremony, known among them as 'eating rice', is observed. It consists in the fathers of the bridegroom and the bride giving each other a handful of rice and swearing that if either thereafter decline to give his son or daughter, as the case may be, in marriage to the daughter or son of the other, as agreed upon, he will have not only to pay the fine to the State but be liable to excommunication. If circumstances do not permit the father of the bride to celebrate the marriage in his own house, he first despatches a goat and three khaṇḍiā (thirty seers) of rice, for a feast of which both the parties are to partake, to the bridegroom's house and, then, accompanies his daughter there. The Padhariyā,* as the priest of the Bāthuris is styled, has to recite the nuptial *mantras*, and both the bride and

* The *padhariyas* have their houses in Daspur, Karanjiā, Māmuriā, Noāgāon, Cilakorhi, Sardā and Vispuri. Those of Adipur have become extinct. Their duties have now devolved upon the Bràhmanas.

the bridegroom wear on the occasion cloths which are tinged with turmeric. But before the couple are finally united in wedlock, yet another ceremony, in the form of an episode, has to be performed. It is what is called by them "guā-paitā"—conferring the sacred thread, with a betel-nut, first upon the bridegroom and then the bride. Here the outward manifestation of the nuptial tie is a thread with some mango-leaves fastened to it, which is tied by the priest round the wrists of both the husband and the wife. When the ceremony is over, the happy couple play with conch-shells. After that the bridegroom cracks his betel-nut of the 'guāpaitā' to pieces and offers a piece to his wife and himself begins to chew another. Then they put on new clothes and go to the house of the former. Here married women perform the ceremony of 'varaṇa,' *i.e.*, they bless and welcome the newly married pair and play various practical jokes upon them. A few days after this the friends and relatives are again invited to a feast in which rice touched by the bride is distributed amongst the guests. This is perhaps the most important feature of the whole marriage ceremony. It is only after this has been done that the bride is really looked upon as a member of her husband's family ; but thereby a restriction is also put upon her: she will never more be allowed to cook food in the house of her father. After she has become a woman she is not allowed to touch any food or drink for seven consecutive days ; on the eighth day she takes a bath, offers worship to the gods and becomes thenceforward entitled to a place in her husband's bed. In the fifth month of her pregnancy the sādha is performed and in the seventh month what is known as kārya bandha.

There was also a peculiarity in their manner of disposing of the dead. When an aged person died, he or she was consigned to the flames; but when the deceased was young, it was the practice to bury the body. The obsequies observed on the two occasions were also different. Before the old man was placed on the funeral pyre, he was covered with a new piece of cloth, a *tulasi* plant was tied round his neck and gold and cows were given away. Ten days were set down as the period of mourning. The chief mourner, whose duty it was to set fire to the pile, and the other relatives of the deceased, were not to touch fish or meat during this period; and it was more particularly enjoined upon the former to have a pure body and a pure mind during this time. He had, besides, on each of these days of mourning to offer as oblations to the manes of the departed, a few sticks and some fried paddy. On the 10th day all the male members of the deceased man's family had to be shaved, the barber being allowed to take away the cloth of the chief mourner. On the 11th day Vaiṣṇavas were feasted with curd and fried rice, and were each given some of the latter uncooked. On the 12th day, to bring the ceremony to a close, the friends and relatives of the dead were fed, and cloths and other presents made to the more respectable guests as marks of honour.

It is alleged by the Bhāthuri Mahāpātras that

it was their ancestors that brought the Bhañja-Rāja family from the west and helped them in establishing themselves in the place of the Virāṭa family. Formerly there were twenty-two zaminders or sāmantas under the Bhañja-Rāja. Four of these were Bāthuris, *viz.*, the zamindars of Simlipāla, Ādipur, Daspur and Karañjia; and they were all honoured with the title of Mahāpātra. They were also each presented by the Bhañja Rājās, with a flag, a silver umbrella and a *chámara*—which they used to display on festive occasions. But all these are now gone, and the families are now trembling on the verge of poverty and ruin, being over head and ears in debt. The poor Bāthuris dragging on their miserable existences in the hills have fallen so low that they look no better than the Kols, the Santāls and other aboriginal tribes. In some places they are even found to observe the rites and manners of the latter ; for instance, they eat hāṇḍiās, domesticate cocks and hens and marry widows. It is for this, we think, that they are regarded by some as descendants of the original non-Aryan inhabitants of the place,* although in reality descended from the ancient Aryan stock. The truth of this would become evident if the appearance and nature of the members of the higher families of the Bāthuri tribe were carefully examined. For the information of the public we give below a representative picture of each of the Daspur and Karañjia families.

* H. H. Risley's Tribes and Castes of Bengal, Vol. I.

Many Bāthuris live also in Keonjhar. They say that in bygone days they exercised a great influence over all the parts of Orissa. Their degeneration and decline commenced in the time of Rājā Pratāparudra. It has been shewn above by extracts from Siddhānta-ḍambara, written four hundred years ago, that in ancient times they and the Brāhmaṇas were upon a footing of equality. Balarāma Dāsa,* the author of the work, says that they used to study the Vedas side by side with the Brāhmaṇas. Since the time of Pratāparudra they have come to be regarded as 'gupta' (krypto, veiled) and unworthy of being touched. Yet they are believed to be in the good books of Viṣṇu or Buddha.

The story of Creation by Çūnya Mahāprabhu and Vedamātā, as narrated by the Bāthuris, closely resembles that told by the Buddhists of the Mahāyāna School. In the Svayambhū Purāṇa of the Buddhists of Nepal, Çūnya Mahāprabhu has been given the name of Svayambhu or Ādi Buddha, and Vedamātā or Ādimātā Dharma or Prajñā. In Siddhānta-ḍambara the *vīja-mantra* of the Bāthuris is said to be "ओं शून्यब्रह्मणे नमः" (Om, salutation to Çūnya-Brahmaṇ). It need hardly be pointed out that this is exactly the *vīja mantra* of the Buddhists of the Mahāyāna School also. Not only this vījā-mantra but the gāyatrī of the

* A detailed account of Balarāma Dāsa and the Buddhists of his time will be given below.

Bāthuris is also to be found in Siddhānta-ḍambara. It runs as follows :—

"ओं सिद्धदेवः सिद्धधर्म्मः वरेण्यमस्य धीमही ।
भर्गदेवो धीयो यो न सिद्धध्रुवो प्रचोदयात् ॥" (Chap. XII)

"Om, let us meditate upon Him, who is self-revealed and self-sustained, who is Siddhadhruva (*i.e.* "the soul of Siddhabhikṣu-saŋgha), who controls and directs our understanding, and who is the only object of adoration by all this animate and inanimate world."

It has been gathered from the lips of an aged *padhariyã* of the Bāthuris that in good old days *gãyatrī* was taken and observed by the great and pious Bāthuris at the time of their initiation into the religious life; but owing to ignorance nobody nowadays cares to practise it.

Just as it was enjoined upon the Buddhists of yore, at the time of their initiation to take the *tricarana-mantra* of "वुद्धं शरणं गच्छामि, धर्म्मं शरणं गच्छामि, सङ्घं शरणं गच्छामि"—"I resign myself to Buddha, I resign myself to Dharma, I resign myself to Saŋgha," so in later times the krypto Buddhists had to take this *gãyatrī*, composed in imitation of the Vedic *gãyatrī*. It goes without saying that this newer form of *gãyatrī* is simply another version of the triçaraṇa-mantra quoted above, its Siddha Deva, Siddha Dharma and Siddha-Dhruva, meaning nothing but Siddhārtha or Buddha, Dharma or Prajñā Pāramitā and Siddha-Saŋgha respectively.

In the remote past the Bāthuris were also known by the name of Bāthula or Bātula. Images of the gods and goddesses worshipped by this people have been disinterred from the ruins of Simlipāla and Ādipurgarh. Amongst these are found images of Acokāntā Mārichi and Prajñā Pāramitā (broken). From the strange combination of the gods and goddesses worshipped by them one might very reasonably consider, they belonged to the class of the Tāntrika Buddhists springing from the Mahāyāna School. A broken image of Prajñā Pāramitā has been preserved in a hut in Ādipur on the banks of the river Baitaraṇī. Under the name of "Bāuri Ṭhākurāṇī" (Bāuri goddess), this image was worshipped by the Padhariyās or priests of the Bāthuris. I learnt from the old "Ḍākuās" of the Mahāpātra family of Dasapurgarh that there was also here a magnificent image of the 'Bāuri Ṭhākuraṇī.' It is only about forty-five years ago that it was taken away by the Dhāruās. In the first chapter of Kaulāvali Tantra we find a reference to another work of the class, called Bātula or Bāthula-tantra. In Madana-Pārijāta* also we find an extract from, it is said, a great tantra named Bāthula. Mahāmahopādhyāya Haraprasād Çāstri has discovered an ancient tāntrika work in Nepal, and refers to it under the name of "Bātula Mahātantra.† Another work of this class, entitled Sarvajñanot-

* *Madana-Parijata* published by the Asiatic Society of Bengal, p. 47.

† H. P. Castri's Nepal Catalogue, p. LXVI.

tara Tantra, and written in the Gupta characters, has also been discovered in Nepal. In this Çiva is the speaker and Saḍānana and Gaṇeça are the listeners. "This was spoken after the completion of the Bāthula-tantra"* The speaker in Siddhānta-ḍambara (from which the origin, the Gāyatrī and the *vījamantra* of the Bāuris have been extracted above,) is also Çiva and the listener Gaṇeça. It is a matter for earnest consideration whether or not the word 'Bāthula' in 'Bāthula-tantra' was in any way connected with the Bāthula or Bāthuri tribe.

Though the Bāthuris had to give up (living as they did, under the sway of Hindu kings, moving in an atmosphere of unlimited influence of the Brāhmaṇas, and labouring under many other untoward circumstances) many of their ancient manners and customs,—nay, though some of them went to the length of renouncing their old religion and are now found offering worship to Rāma and Mahāvīra, yet their faith has not been wholly shaken, nor have they entirely given up their ancient beliefs and prejudices. They still worship Dharmarāja and Jagannātha who is popularly known as Buddha. In some places they are also found paying the homage of their heart to Çūnya-Brahman (vulgarly known as Baḍām).

* H. P. Cāstri's Nepal Catalogue, p. Lxxiv.

CHAPTER III.

BUDDHISM IN THE 16TH CENTURY.

In dwelling upon the history of the *Bāthuris* we have attempted to throw a sidelight upon the existence of a Buddhistic Society in the backward districts of the several Gaḍajāts. We have then hinted that even so far back as the 16th century, although in its fallen condition, Buddhism was a *prevalent and highly influential* creed in Utkal, influencing the thoughts and lives and purifying the hearts and minds of many thousands of her neglected children outwardly professing other creeds. This side-hint, we are conscious, must have raised, in the minds of thoughtful and inquisitive seekers after truth and knowledge, such questions as, how could the religion of Gautama-Buddha have for centuries held its own under the terrible persecutions of the bigoted Brahmanas and the no less bigoted Hindu kings; how were these mute votaries of the Mahāyāna faith able to hoodwink the argus-eyed Brahmanas and their followers, and inwardly cherish a loving memory of the defunct creed and offer the incense of their loyal devotion at the altar of their god enshrined in the recesses of their hearts; how and where were these unknown and unrecognised little bands of crypto Buddhists maintaining their ground, suffering, as they did, innumerable tortures and persecutions, and driven further and further beyond the pale of civilization and society?—These questions and many more must have presented themselves to every student of the history of the Bāthuri tribe; so we shall take this opportunity to solve them in the light of the records which we have been fortunate enough to rescue from the jealous clutch of concealment or oblivion.

The names of Achyutānanda Dāsa, Balarāma Dāsa, Jagannātha Dāsa, Ananta Dāsa and Yaçovanta Dāsa are held in high esteem by the pious Vaiṣṇavas of Utkala—so much so that they have almost come to be household words with them. Besides these, there was also another, equally famous and equally honoured, *viz.*, Chaitanya Dāsa. These six are the principal poets who, with hearts stirred by religious fervour, sang the glories of Çrī Kṛṣṇa, and have, in consequence, been generally regarded (although, wrongly, as we shall show hereafter) as interpreters and champions of Vaiṣṇavism in Utkal. The pious-poet Achyutānanda has left us an immortal effusion in his Çūnya Saṁhita. From this we learn that he flourished in the Nīlāchala in the reign of King Pratāparudra of Utkal, about the same time as Chaitanya. Here we also find mention of Balarāma Dāsa, Jagannātha Dāsa, Ananta Dāsa and Yaçovanta Dāsa,* as his contemporaries. But nowhere does he refer to

---

Cunya Samhitā, Chap X.

the illustrious Chaitanya Dāsa. This fact, together with the unmistakable sketch that the latter has drawn of himself in his Nirguṇa Māhātmya,* leads us to believe that he was not their contemporary but flourished shortly after them, and before the reign of Pratāparudra had drawn to a close. It is in any case beyond doubt that by the presence of all these six *Dāsas* (lit., followers or servants)† Utkal was honoured and sanctified early in the beginning of the 16th century.

We have already remarked that these six great souls, permeated through and through with love and devotion towards their Maker, are generally recognised as the principal Vaiṣṇava poets of Utkal, and their works regarded as the principal Vaiṣṇava literature of the country. But we hope and trust we shall be able to make good, from their own utterances, the fact that though they outwardly professed the Vaiṣṇava faith and propagated the Chaitanya cult, yet in their heart of hearts they were but sincere and staunch pioneers and champions of the long neglected, and almost forgotten, religion of the Mahāyāna School.

---

* Nirguna Māhātmya, Chap. XVI.

† The word 'Dāsa' means here 'one who has known Brahman as he —a Brahmajnāni. Thus we find in Cunya Samhitā—

"नामतत्त्व चिह्नि आत्मातत्त्वज्ञानी नामब्रह्म यार आश।
ब्रह्मदर्शी सहि अवश्य अटइ प्रभुङ्कर सेहि दास॥" १६ अ:।

—He only, who has known the secret of *namu* as well as the secret of the soul, ego, and has rested all his hopes in Brahman as represented by *name*, is the real seer of Brahman and can only be said to be the staunch and faithful follower or servant (Dāsa) (of the lord).

In his noble work, the Virāṭagītā, Balarāma Dāsa who is regarded as the foremost among these, puts the following lines, expressive of the tenets of the author, into the mouth of Arjuna, while speaking to Çrī Kṛṣṇa—

"तोहर रूप रेख नाहो। शून्यपुरुष शून्यदेहो॥
बोइलि शून्य तोर देहो। आवर नाम थिव कांहों॥
शून्यरे ब्रह्मसिना थाहि। सेठारे नाम थिव रहि॥"

"Thou hast no form or figure. Thou art but the void personified and embodied. Though possessed of a body, thee I know to be Çūnya, Void. How couldst thou have other names? Brahman dwells in Çūnya, where there is nothing but name, *i.e.*, sound."

These lines, if properly construed, can hardly mean anything but a clear enunciation of the doctrine of Çūnya which is the kernel of the Mahāyāna Buddhism.

Further on we again hear Arjuna say :—

"तोर शून्यरूप शून्यदेह। किना दैत्यारि नामव्यूह॥"

"Çūnya, the Void, is thy form; Çūnya is thy body. How is it then that thou art carrying the name of (*i.e.* art called) Daityāri, Extirpator of Demons?"

And in reply to this, Çrī Kṛṣṇa himself is made to say :—

"मोहर शून्यरे विश्राम। से ठारे कहु अच्छि नाम॥
मोतो सन्देह लागिला। कांहुतो नाम जात हेला॥"

विराटगीता।

"Çūnya is my resting-place, *i.e.*, when I give up this image, I become identified with Çūnya; and that is, I say, my real name. I am also puzzled to think how and where the name (you speak of) was given to me."

Not only in Virāṭagītā, but in all his works we meet with clear and unmistakable proofs of his belief in the Great Void as being the origin and the end of all the created world. Upon this one point is founded the whole fabric of his theology and religion. Thus in his Brahmāṇḍa-Bhūgola-Gītā, we find Çrī Kṛṣṇa giving the following description of himself to Arjuna :—

"केहि न थिलै हे अर्ज्जुन। महाशून्यरे मोर जन्म ॥"

"There was none (prior to me) O Arjuna. I owe this life of mine to the Great Void, *i.e.*, I came out of it, or I am one with it."

At length in the maŋgalācharaṇa of his Sārasvata-Gītā, Balarāma Dāsa delivers himself of the following prayer to the Maker—

"जय धर्म्म श्री पुरुषोत्तम। अनादि स्तुति परमब्रह्म ॥ १
अव्यक्त पुरुष निराकार हरि। सर्व्व घटे अच्छु ब्रह्मरूप धरि ॥ २
नाहि रेख रूप तोर श्रीविश्वपुरुष। विषु र गोचर होइछु प्रकाश ॥ ३
मन-नयन-चित-चेतन नाहि तोर। कर्म्म धर्म्म सर्व्व ठारे सिद्ध न कर ॥ ४
महाशून्य तोर नाम। ओंकार शब्द एजे वेदान्त आगम ॥ ५"

(१म अध्याय।)

"All glory to thee, the soul of religion, the blessed First Being. I pray to thee, the self-sustained, Brahman of Brahmans. Ye unrevealed Person, O Hari (the Destroyer of all troubles and cares), O Lord, thou hast no form, no body. Yet thou art existent inside all bodies, assuming the forms of their souls. O Mighty Omniscient Being, having no form, no image, Thou dost yet reveal thyself to Viṣṇu. Thou art destitute of the mind, the eyes (the senses), the heart, and consciousness, and thou art always above and independent of all works and all religious observances and practices. Thou art (appropriately) styled the Great Void or Cypher. We learn from the Vedānta, that the letter ओं first originated in the void."

—An exposition of the Divine Power, wholly after the doctrine of Buddhism! He is not described as a cypher in the sense of being an airy nothing, but as the essence, the total abstraction, of all powers and activities. God is not a whit denied; on the contrary He is acknowledged to be the origin and the soul of all existence. The drift of these lines is clearly this—God is Nature suspended.

That this was the cardinal principle of his religion is further proved, if further proof be necessary, by the following words that Çrī Kṛṣṇa is made to say to Arjuna in the same work (a little below the benedictory preface)—

"श्रीहरि वोईले हो शुण पाण्डुसुत ।
ब्रह्ममहिमा तोते कहिबा वेदान्त ॥
महाशून्यकु जे ब्रह्म बोलि कहि । ।
से ब्रह्मरूप होइला निरञ्जन देही ॥

निरञ्जन ठाकु हैला परम अवतार।
परम ठाकु जीव हैइला बाहार॥"

मारस्वतगीता १म अध्याय।

"Çrī Kṛṣṇa said 'Hear me, O son of Pāṇḍu. I shall tell you in detail of the glories of Brahman. The Great Void which is said to be Brahman, (once) assumed the form of a *human being* (Nirañjana). And thus (out of the Great Void) came out a grand and glorious Being."

Thus is the theory of incarnation of the Great Void maintained and explained by these veiled followers of Buddha, largely influenced, as they were, by the religion of Çrī Chaitanya.

From the above extracts it is evident that the Çrī Kṛṣṇa and Brahman of Balarāma Dāsa is absolutely one and the same with his Mahā-Çūnya, Çūnya-Puruṣa and Nāma. All that can be said in defence of those who regarded these pious and devout souls as Vaiṣṇava poets is that their religious lives and views were moulded and regulated, to a considerable extent, by the preachings of the Vaiṣṇava masters. And no wonder, considering the atmosphere they breathed and the pressure brought to bear upon them. Besides, the want of a living example and influence of the Buddhistic faith in their midst helped the Vaiṣṇava creed to gain tho uppor hand in regulating their faith.

Thus we find Jagannātha Dāsa expressing himself in his Tulā-bhinā—

"सकल मन्त्र तीर्थ ज्ञान। वीइल शून्य ये प्रमाण॥ (p. 20.)
येते कहिलुं गो पार्ब्बती। ए सर्ब्बे शून्यरे अछन्ति॥ (p, 20.)
महाशून्यरु शून्य जात। से शून्य प्रणव सम्भूत॥
प्रणव परमकु कहि। सकल शास्त्र ये वोलाइ॥" (p. 21.)

"The drift and aim of all *mantras*, pilgrimages and knowledge points to the validity of Çūnya."

"All those that I have spoken to you of, O Pārvati, do but dwell in (*i.e.*, are but manifestations of) the Void."

"Out of the Great Void came the Void : and from the Void itself came Praṇava (Oṁ), which is said by all the Çāstras, to be the Parama, the Finalê."

Chaitanya Dāsa also says in his Nirguṇa Māhātmya—

"आत्मा पुरुष भगवान। आत्मा उपरे ताकु चिन॥ १८०
ए आत्मा परे अछि ब्रह्म। चिह्निले छिण्डइ बन्धन॥ १८२
ए देह गले ब्रह्म याइ। महाशून्यरे विश्रामइ॥ १८३
से आत्मा ब्रह्मकु जगिछि। बान्धि थोइला प्राये अछि॥ १८४
निरञ्जन छाड़ि गले प्राण। से पद एव महाशून्य॥ १८५
शून्यपुरुष सङ्गे थिव। खोंजिले आउ न पाइव॥" १८६

१६श अध्याय।

"Ātmā Puruṣa, the soul, is the Bhagavat (the repository of all attributes). But know Him (the

Nirguṇa) to be above and independent of the soul, *i.e.*, the attributes. Brahman is above this Ātman; by knowing Him all the worldly ties are cut asunder. After leaving this body, we go to, and mix up with, Brahman, and rest (eternally) in the Great Void. The soul is ever conscious of, and living in, Brahman and is as though smarting under the (physical) restraints. When the life will depart from the body, the body will become Mahā-Çūnya. (But) I shall live on in the Çūnya-Puruṣa, never to be found even after careful searches."

We find from the above that Chaitanya Dāsa's Nirguṇa-puruṣa clearly means a total abstraction of all phenomenal activities. His Nirguṇa does not mean 'devoid of attributes,' but *above and independent of* attributes, of which the worlds are but manifestations.

Achyutānanda Dāsa's treatment of this doctrine of Çūnya in his Çūnya-Saṁhitā is more lucid and more philosophical. His Çūnya Puruṣa is the only actor on the illusory stage of the world. He observes :—

"भला पचारिलु गुपत सन्धि । शून्यपुरुप शून्य परे वन्दी ॥
शून्यपुरुष उदासरे रहे । शून्यपुरुष सवु माया भ्यायी ॥
शून्यपुरुष दयालु घटइ । शून्यपुरुष सर्ब्बघटे रहि ॥
शून्यपुरुष करे नट घट । शून्यपुरुष जाणे छन्दकूट ॥
शून्यपुरुष शून्यरे मारइ । मारि शून्य पुणा गति करइ ॥

"The hidden mystery (of creation) has been well laid bare to me. (It is this). The Çūnya Purașa has become (as it were) a prisoner in

Çūnya. Though He is the master of all these illusions, having power to spread and draw them in, yet He Himself is quite indifferent to, and keeps Himself quite aloof from, all these. He is exceedingly kind, being always anxious to free us from the influence of Māyā and dwells inside every created thing. From here He, well versed in craft and cunning, stirs up all the differences and discords (out of sheer kindness, so that we may not lose Him in the illusions). And when in the course of these one murders another, it is really He who murders Himself (the same Çūnya Puruṣa being inside both the murderer and the murdered) and frees the murdered from all bondage and gives him the reward of a happy emancipation."

Then he goes on to describe mystically how the Çūnya Puruṣa as Jīvātman has created a world of bondage for himself and how he is reigning there

"शून्य मन्त्रे शून्यपुरुष धरा । दण्ड थाइ राजा होइण त्वरा ॥
शून्य पुरुष आपे दण्डि होए । सर्ब्बदोष बाधा न याइ चयी ॥
शून्य पुरुषकु कीते भगारि । मारिबा इच्छा अटइ ताहारि ॥
शून्य पुरुष वेढ़िछि वेढ़रे । शत शान्ति दया चमा पाशरे ॥
एकादश इन्द्र बेढ़ि अछन्ति । काम क्रोध मोह द्वार जागन्ति ॥
द्वादश दलाइ गडनायक । पचिश प्रकृति पञ्च मनत ॥
षड चक्ररे पञ्चाश अचर । बाहत्तरि नाड़ी से गड पाशर ॥
गड चारि पाशे एमाने द्वारी । शून्य पुरुषकु थान्ति आवरि ॥
शून्य पुरुषरे एतेक तेज । शून्य होइ भोग्य करइ राज्य ॥
शून्य पुरुष अलगी रहिछि । शून्य परे रहि लीला करुछि ॥

न छुअन्ति ताकु पचिश जण । अलगी रहि करे भिन्ना भिन्न ॥
शून्य पुरे शून्य पुरुष रहे । शून्य भजन निराकार ध्याये ॥
बाविंश अचरे करे भजन । शून्य पुरुष निराकारध्यान ॥"

"Çūnya Puruṣa can be taken only through the Çūnya Mantra. He is a king with all the emblems of royalty. (These emblems do, however, mean but restraints put upon himself); and such is the strength and force of these restraints and bonds, the sources of all evils, that though lord of them all, He cannot shake them off. He has innumerable opponents and enemies, and is very anxious to free Himself from them. With goodness, mercy, love of peace and forgiveness, about him, He is passing his days, as it were, inside a dungeon, always trying to get out and always opposed. Lust, passion and (mental) infatuation are keeping watch at the gate ; and twelve watchmen are in charge of the fortification. The twenty-five causes, the five minds, the six mystic circles of the body and the fifty letters, and the seventy-two veins and arteries—all these are mounting guard near and about the fortification. By these sentries the Çūnya Puruṣa is surrounded on all sides. O how great is the prowess of the Çūnya Puruṣa !—Though a pure and simple abstraction, yet He is exercising all the rights of royalty. He is, however, quite aloof from all these, and only diverts Himself thus—in no way affected or polluted by them. He is not within the reach of the twenty-five causes, rather He creates differences among them from afar. The Çūnya Puruṣa is living, as it were, inside a Çūnya castle, praying to, and meditating upon, the imageless Çūnya, by means of the thirty-two letters."......

These lines, however crude the philosophy underlying them, mean that the Çūnya Puruṣa, living within ourselves as our soul or Ego, can be realised only if we can throw off the shackles of nature and her concomitant fears and temptations ; and that, though living within us, He is no party to any of our natural propensities and can be reached only by annihilating the mind and resting all our thoughts upon Him as Çūnya Puruṣa.

Then he clearly and unhesitatingly rejects the accepted forms of worship, and formulates others which will be hailed as bright and undying sparks from the great fire of Buddhism. His words are :—

"अखद ब्रह्माण्ड उपरे अछि । शून्य शून्य महाशून्यरे गच्छि ॥
निराकार भजि मा दुर्गा देवी । एणु निर्लेपकु थायान्ति सेवि ॥
तु ये पचारिलु परम सन्धि । ध्यान धारणा आदिमान विधि ॥
अङ्गन्यास करन्यास हिं नाहिं । स्थानभङ्ग मुद्रा किच्छिहिं नाहिं ॥
ऊर्द्धकर योड़ि कर तु लये । ऊर्द्धमुख करि कर तुलए ॥
ऊर्द्धमुख करि चित्ताकु ध्याअ । विकूट सन्धि अलेखकु चाहँ ॥
निराकार मन्त्र कण्ठ चक्ररे । वील वाव् स्वर ऊर्द्ध मुखरे ॥
द्वाविंश अक्षर उच्चार कर । नयन न चलु चित्ता अक्षर ॥
अचलि येसने मन्दर रहे । अचलि तेसने ज्योतीन्द्र ध्याये ॥
अचलि सुमन निश्चल धर । शून्यपुरुषकु तु लये कर ॥
दिशिव शून्य दिव्यमान काया । निराकाररूप अरूपदेहा ॥"

(शून्यसंहिता ७म अ:)

"He is above the fourteen worlds; and being himself void goes up to the Great Void. Mother Durgā is worshiping the Formless and is always engaged in praying to the *Nirlepa*, the Absolute. Thou hast laid bare the deepest and most valuable secret. We do now know that the religious injunctions of meditation, steady mental abstraction and the like, the touching of certain parts of the body and certain gesticulations of the hands in worship, the peculiar intertwining of the fingers for the same purpose,—all these are absolutely void and meaningless. We have only to fold our hands together and to lift them up, palms upwards, and with the face decorated with the sacred marks on the forehead and turned up towards the heaven, to offer our prayers. The muttering of set prayers, the telling of the beads of the rosary, are all done away with; and we have, instead, only to look inward—within ourselves. With upturned face, we have to utter the Çūnya *mantra* from the mystic circle in the throat. And this *mantra* is nothing but to utter the thirty-two letters, with the eyes fixed upon the circle midway between the eyebrows. When the temple of the body will be motionless, then has the motionless lord of all lustres to be meditated upon. Then the mind has to be made firm and steady and fixed upon and absorbed in the Çūnya Puruṣa. Then will you see the bright and beautiful Çūnya form of Him who has no form, no figure and yet has a body."

Although professing to be Vaiṣṇavas, they interpret the cult of Rādhā-Kṛṣṇa in a new way, and one quite different from the ordinary

Vaiṣṇava point of view. The following extract from the writings of Achyutānanda and Jagannātha will show how under the veil of Vaiṣṇavism this sect propagates in reality some of the doctrines of the Mahāyāna School :—

(*a*) "जीव आत्मा राधे वलि परम मुरारि ।" (शून्यसंहिता २य अ: ।)

Rādhikā is the Jīvātman and Murāri the Paramātman.

(*b*) "एकाङ्ग ब्रह्मरूप होइ। राधिका सङ्गे भावग्राही ॥
गोलक नित्य एहा कहि। शून्य देउल ए बोलाई ॥"

" One and the same with Rādhikā, as being part and parcel of the same body, Brahman, approachable only through the heart, resides in Golaka which is nothing but the Çunyadeul or void." (Jagannātha in his Tulābhinā.)

(*c*) "परम आत्माटी महाशून्य वलि भाव ।
एहिटि अरूपानन्द नाम तत्त्व ठुल ।
छइव संग्रह करि राधा प्रेम भील ॥"

" Know the Paramātman to be the Mahā-Çūnya. Know him, in short, to be the formless source of bliss, to be nothing but the name itself." (Çūnya Saṁhita, Ch. 22.)

Here Achyutānanda makes a clearer statement of his doctrines. Hence it is evident that the interpretation given to the cult of Rādhā-Kṛṣṇa by these writers does not at all tally with the mythological accounts of the Vaiṣṇavas. The whole subject has been idealised and elaborated in such a way as to signify the relations of man's soul to Paramātman. Jagannātha Dāsa has openly declared that Vṛndāvana, Mathurā and other holy places should not be localised on any map or identified with the actual villages of the same names. In reality they signify Mahā-Çūnya or the Great Void :—

"कृष्णर क्रीड़ारस एहि। गुपत वृन्दावन कहि॥
मथुरापुर महाशून्य। गोपनगर सेहु जान॥"

—"Such is the meaning of the love-feats of Kṛṣṇa. Vṛndāvana is really a secret place. Mathurāpura means nothing but the Great Void, and this is also the meaning of Gopanagara."

(Tulābhinā, Ch. 9.)

The following extract from Brahmāṇḍa-Bhūgola-Gītā of Balarāma Dāsa reads like another version of the origin of the universe given by Rāmāi Paṇḍit* during the ascendancy of the Pāla Kings :—

"ये काले न थिला संसार। न थिला चन्द्र दिवाकर।
न थिले दिवस रजनी। न थिला मेद मेदा भूमि॥
न थिले थावर पवन। न थिले शून्य तारागण॥
न थिले देवासुर नर। न थिले संसार सागर॥
न थिले अल्प तेज वल। न थिले ब्रह्मा विष्णु हर॥
से काले शून्य मोर रूप। एमन्ते गला कोटिकल्प॥
ब्रह्माण्ड मोर गर्भे लेहि। रखिलि ब्रह्मरूप होइ॥

केहि न थिलि हे अर्ज्जुन ।	महाशून्यरूप मोर जन्म ।
एमन्ते केते दिन अन्ते ।	दया बसिला मोर चित्ते ॥
सृष्टि करिते वाञ्छा हेला ।	मो अङ्ग विन्दु उछलिला ॥
से विन्दु हस्तरे ठेलि ।	त्रि अङ्गुलि गलाइलि ॥
से विन्दु त्रिय भाग हेला ।	त्रिबीज रस बलाइला ॥
त्रिबीजरु त्रिय देव ।	होइले ब्रह्मा विष्णु शिव ॥"

—"When the world was not in existence, when there was neither the sun nor the moon, neither day nor night, neither land nor water, neither the fixed earth nor the inconstant wind, nor were there the sky and the stars in it, when there was no god, no demon, no human being; when there was no world, no ocean, no force, no fire; when there was no Brahmā, Viṣṇu or Hara, then was Çūnya my form, and thus did crores of kalpas pass away. Then did I assume the form of Brahman with the Brahmāṇḍa inside me. There was none, O Arjuna, (to bring me out). I came out of the Great Void. After a pretty long time had thus passed away, my heart was moved and I felt inclined to create the world. Then out of my person did seed begin to ooze. I brushed it off with three fingers of my hand. The seed, thus brushed off, became divided into three parts, charged with three different qualities and out of these three parts of the seed did the three gods of Brahmā, Viṣṇu and Çiva come."

In his Gaṇeça-Vibhūti-ṭīkā, we find Balarāma Dāsa attempting at a description of his Çūnya Puruṣa. He says

"अनाकाररूपं शून्यं शून्यं मध्ये निरञ्जनः ।
निराकारमङ्गज्योतिः सज्योतिर्भगवानयम् ॥"

"The Çūnya is devoid of all forms and shapes. In the centre of this Çūnya is Nirañjana, a formless and brilliant figure. It is that shapeless and formless brilliant figure which is Bhagavat, the master of all attributes."

Achyuta Dāsa in his Çūnya-Saṁhitā, Anādi-Saṁhitā, and Anākāra Saṁhitā, uses the terms 'Anākāra,' 'Nirākāra', 'Nirañjana', 'Ajara', 'Anādya' and 'Akṣaya' as synonymous with the term Çūnya; and these terms have always been employed to describe the indescribable Divine Being. But he has not, like the other Buddhistic preachers of this age, been completely able to shake off the belief in the gods and goddesses as intermediate beings between man and Çūnya. He exclaims:

"बोलन्ति गुरु शुण व्रजसुत, कहिबा तोते बुझाइ।
प्रथमरे गुरु विद्या पढ़ावन्ति ब्रह्मभाग दूरे थोई॥
ब्रह्मा विष्णु रुद्र ता परे दुर्गाये पड़ान्ति आदेर गुरु।
साम जजु रक् अथर्व्व ए आदि पड़ान्ति आद्य ठाकुर।"

"Guru, the spiritual preceptor, says—Hear me, O Vrajasuta, I shall explain (it) to you in detail. Aim, at the outset, at a knowledge of the Guru, leaving aside all attempts at an acquisition of the knowledge of the Brahman. Know Brahmā, Viṣṇu, Rudra and Durgā as the first preceptors, being embodiments of the different attributes of the Godhead, and you will gradually learn of the primitive Thākura, the first and foremost God, by studying the Sāma, Yajūs, Rik and Atharva Vedas."

But his highly spiritual culture convinced him of the uselessness of merely studying books, and he draws a nice distinction between the mere reading of them and an intelligent assimilation of the principles therein laid down with the whole head and heart. The mind will have to be annihilated, and only those principles which help us in identifying ourselves with the Brahman, should be scrupulously observed.

"कोड़िये गुटियेः फला पढ़ालि रज तमे मन रखि।
ब्रह्मर भेद तहि किछि न पाइ कर्म्ममार्गे मन जगि॥" ६८

" You have learnt, although not without great trouble, the alphabets of religion and the words produced by their permutations and combinations, whilst your mind was completely under the influence and control of the lower attributes of ignorance and passion. These attributes, as opposed to the third and highest attribute, *viz.*, Sattva, *i.e.*, the spiritualistic tendency, drag us down and keep us bound to the way of karman, work, for salvation. So having the mind absorbed in work (materialism), you have not been able to find the real nature of the Brahman."

"गीता भागवत पुराण पढ़िवा कहिबा चातुरी थिव।
तत्त्व अनाकार नाम ब्रह्मभेद न पाई व्यर्थे हेव॥" १०२

(अनाकारसंहिता)

"(Unless you are bent upon the salvation of your soul) you will read the Gītā, the Bhāgavata, the Purāṇas and yet learn nothing but tricks and cunning (to impose upon the worldly-minded people). All your pains will be fruitless. You will know nothing of the mystery of the conception of Godhead as devoid of all forms and images, which means a complete unification and identification of the *name* and the conception of Brahman."

It is evident from these lines that Achyuta Dāsa laid no stress upon the study of the Hindu religious çāstras. We may study them as much as we like and yet be not a whit improved. Until and unless we thoroughly digest the knowledge that Brahman is absolutely nirākāra and is wholly identical with the nāma itself, we shall be grovelling in the darkness of ignorance and passion. It is also doubtful whether he had any faith in the Brāhmanic customs, though he had not been completely able to rid himself of allegiance to them.

At the end of his work he refers to the scriptures, the main themes of which, he says, are to sing the glories of Çrī Kṛṣṇa; and his own Anākāra-Saṁhitā is simply an epitome of all these. Moreover, the Çrī Kṛṣṇa of these scriptures is not the Çrī Kṛṣṇa of Vaiṣṇavism: it is a pure and simple pseudonym, so to speak, for the Anākāra Çūnya Puruṣa of Buddhism, adopted, as appears likely, to throw dust in the eyes of the jealous Brāhmaṇas. Except for occasional glimpses, to be found in his works, of the spiritual region of the class of thinkers to which he belongs, we have no other proofs to establish their faith in Buddhism. It is for this that they have generally passed for devout Vaiṣṇavas. But to any careful student of religion these glimpses will be quite sufficient to illumine the whole course of their religious tendency. Thus he says :—

"अनाकार जे श्रीब्रह्मसंहिता ग्रन्थ मने कर सार ।
श्रीकृष्णचरणे शरण पशिला दीन अच्युत पामर ॥
छत्तिश संहिता अष्टोत्तर गीता वंशानुसप्तवासरे ।
उपवंशानु द्वाविंशखण्ड घेनि भविष्य तेर खण्डरे ॥
पद पदावली लक्ष लक्ष ग्रन्थ सबु श्रीकृष्णमहिमा ।
तो आगे कहिलूँ व्रजकुमार ब्रह्मसारस्वतसीमा ॥
ए अध्याय गुपत करिण रखिलु वेलरे हेब प्रकाश ।
श्रीकृष्णचरणे शरण पशिला पामर अच्युतदास ॥
व्रजकुल तारि आपणे तरिवि श्रीकृष्णसहाय हेइछि ।
अव्यक्त हरि अनाकार पूरि तेणु पद पुरु अछि ॥"

"Only do think of (*i.e.*, firmly adhere to the injunction laid down in) the Great Brahma-Saṁhitā which deals with the Anākāra. And with this advice to you all, the low and sinful Achyuta Dāsa (meaning himself) resigns himself absolutely to the grace of Çrī Kṛṣṇa. All the scriptures, *viz.*, the thirty-six Saṁhitās, the hundred and eight Gītās and the seven series of the Vaṁçānucharita, the twenty-two volumes of the Upa-Vaṁçanucharita and the thirteen volumes of the Bhaviṣya, all the religious hymns and songs and lyrics, and hundreds of thousands of other books,—all sing the glory of Çrī Kṛṣṇa. O son of Vraja (*i.e.*, devotee of Çrī Kṛṣṇa), I have already told you of the subject-matter of Brahma-Sārasvata-Gītā. But this chapter (meaning probably a full discussion of Çrī Kṛṣṇa) has been kept secret from you—only to be divulged hereafter. And now the mean and humble Achyuta Dāsa bids adieu to you taking refuge at the feet of Çrī Kṛṣṇa (*i.e.*, resigning himself to His grace). And now, through His grace, not only he, but the whole line of Vraja-Sutas, will be saved. In the realm of Anākāra dwells the unrevealed Hari, and Achyuta has thrown himself completely at His mercy."

From the above quotation, it is clear that this class of Vaiṣṇava poets did not attach much importance, if any at all, to the Vedas and the Purāṇas of the Hindus. They had their own scriptures, composed by the highest and greatest amongst them; and a scrupulous adherence to the injunctions and principles here enunciated they considered a better passport for the attainment of Mokṣa.

However veiled the religious views of these poets may have been generally, they, sometimes, out of the fulness of their hearts, allow the expression of their faith to flow in clear and limpid streams. Thus in his Viṣṇu-garbha, we find Chaitanya Dāsa saying :—

"अगोचर पुरुष से नाहि रूपवर्ण ।
पृथिवि नाहि तार अटे महाशून्य ॥
रूपवर्ण न होई से अरूप तार देही ।
शून्यर सङ्गते से शून्य होई थाई ॥
अरूप अवर्ण से लक्ष्य देवाकु नीहिव उपमा ।
चौद्द ब्रह्माण्ड खोजिले नाहि प्रतिसीमा ॥

प्रति तुल्य लच्य सेःन भासिलं कांदि ।
एमन्त महिमा से भलेखर देहो ॥
शून्य सङ्गते से शून्य शून्य शून्यरूपी ।
शून्य सङ्गते मिशि भछि सकल स्थानव्यापी ।
शून्य हिंटि ताहार भठई निजघर ।
शून्यरे थाई से शून्ये करई वेहार ॥"

"Devoid of all forms and figures, He is no subject of experience. There is nothing beyond or above Him in the whole of the Mahāçūnya."

"He has no form, no colour. His body may be said to be the absence of all forms and structures. He is Çūnya, being one and the same with Çūnya."

"He is devoid of all forms and destitute of all colours; amongst the thousand and one gods there is none to be any match for Him. Search the whole of the fourteen worlds but nowhere will you find any limit to Him. Even hundreds of thousands of gods will be no whit of a rival for Him—so great is the glory and greatness of that Formless Person. He is mixed up with Çūnya, He is Çūnya, His form is Çūnya, and identified with Çūnya, He is ever over the whole of space."

"His proper home is in Çūnya; and dwelling in Çūnya He makes Himself manifest in Çūnya."

What more convincing proof of their staunch faith in Buddhism can one expect? Here the author has risen above all dread of persecution, and, for once at least, makes bold to announce himself clearly, and without the least shade of ambiguity, as embracing the doctrine of the Void.

But the above are not the only passages that betray these krypto Buddhists. In their scriptures numberless pebbles of faith lie on the shore, and one has only to pick up and examine a few to know that they are but fragments of the mighty Buddhistic structure.

Balarāma Dāsa thus expounds the theory in his Brahmāṇḍa-Bhugola-gītā by way of an address to Arjuna.—

"Listen, O Arjuna, with attention—I am going to explain to you (the principles of) the Bhāgavata. Out of the Great Void came the Void and out of this came *moha*, illusion." (Chap. II). "That which is called *nigama* is in reality the Great Void. It is simply because the end of the Vedas cannot be reached, that they were given the name of Nigama. That which is called *Kalpataru* (lit. a tree bearing, as its fruits, the objects of our desires), is really an embodiment of the Formless !"[1]

---

1 "शुण अर्जुन मन देइ। कहिबा भागवत फेड़॥
महाशून्यरू शून्य हेला। से शून्य फल मोह हेला॥"
(२य अध्याय।)

"निगम बोलि जाहा कहि। महाशून्यटी से अटइ॥
वेद अंहि कि न गमिला। तेणु निगम नाम हेला॥
कलपतरुटी जाहा कहि। निराकारटी रूप सेहि॥
से ठारु रस बीज गलि। से रस बीज फल फलि॥
पुण बोलि ता [illegible] कहि। सुभा रमटी से अटइ॥"
(४र्थ अध्याय।)

The above quotations from the great poets of the 16th century leave little room for doubt that Mahāçūnya, the Great Void, which is the cardinal doctrine of the Mādhyamika Philosophy, was also the highest goal of their religious aspirations. It is indeed the case that we very frequently meet with such words of Hindu Philosophy as Bhāgavata, Nigama, Jñānatattva, Haribhakti, Kṛṣṇa-kathā and others in their works; the most casual student of these will, however, admit that belief in Mahāçūnya, the Great Void, is still the mainspring of their religious life. Balarāma Dāsa himself has unmistakably hinted that there is nothing of any value whatsoever in mere nomenclature. His point is, whatever name we may apply, we always refer to one and the same Supreme Being, conceivable in the form of Oṁ and identical with Çūnya Brahman. It is for this reason that the pious Vaiṣṇava poets are found frequently to allude to the name as the sole essence of the universe. Balarāma Dāsa gives the following account of himself in his Guptagītā or Chattiçā—

"Highly pleased to hear this, Arjuna fell prostrate at the feet of Çrī Kṛṣṇa and said 'How will the occult Guptagītā be made known? Be pleased, O my Lord, to tell me through whose lips you will make it public. Çrī Hari answered, "Hear me O Arjuna. I have a favourite son (disciple) named Paduma. He will have a son under the name of Aniruddha. He will, in his turn, pass away in course of time. I, who am known in the Vedas as Brahman Himself, will in the Kaliyuga, assume the form of Dāru-Brahma (Jagannātha). There will then be a king under the name of Pratāparudra. In his time from Somanātha will descend Aniruddha by his wife Jamunā. In one of the chapters of Guptagītā it is given out that he will be named Balarāma Dāsa, through whose lips, says Balarāma Dāsa, will pour out the nectar of the precepts of the Guptagītā."[1]

The following lines, also from his Praṇava Gītā,* are well deserving of quotation in this connection:—

"The Brāhmaṇas listened attentively to my discussion of the principles of the Praṇava Gītā, which are in reality the occult principles of the

---

1 "शुणि अर्ज्जुन त्दपुति हइला। चरणतले पड़ि पचारिला ॥ ४२
गुपतगीता ये होइछि गुपत। कलिरे केमन्ते हेव उकत ॥ ४३
काहा मुखरे एहा कहाइब। ए कथा प्रभु मोते आज्ञा हेव ॥ ४४
श्रीहरि बोइले शुण अर्ज्जुन। पदुम अटइ मोर नन्दन ॥ ४५
ताहार सुत अनिरुध हेव। से पुणि कालरे चय होइव ॥ ४६
मु ये बेवरु ब्रह्म अवतार। कलियुगे दारुब्रह्मशरीर ॥ ४७
प्रतापरुद्र नामे हेव राए। कहइ तोते से काल संशये ॥ ४८
सोमनाथ नामे पुत्र ताहार। अनिरुध जात ताहार घर ॥ ४९
जमुना नामे ताहार भारिया। अनिरुध हेव ताहार तनुजा ॥ ५०
ताहार नाम वलराम दास। गुपतगीता अध्याये प्रकाश ॥ ५१
वलरामदास गुपत करि। अध्याय करि सेहु निवे मरि ॥ ५२
ता मुखे कहाइवा गीतारस। भावरे भणिले वलरामदास ॥" ५३

(२५ण अध्याय ।)

* In some MSS. the name is Pralamba-Gitā.

Gītā based upon the Vedānta Çāstra, from upon the *Mukti-mandapa.* But when they found that it was I who had done this, ceaseless was the torrent of abuse that poured upon me. Even Mahārāja Pratāparudra scolded me severely in great wrath and said "What right have you, a Çūdra, to utter the Praṇava (Oṁ) and discuss the principles of the Vedas? Certainly it is wrong on your part to do so." Hearing this I smiled gently and said "Hear me, O protector of men and master of elephants,—Çrīpati (lit., husband of Çrī, goddess of good fortune, *i.e.*, Bhagavat) is in no body's exclusive possession (as birth-right). He is his who is a good and pious man—be he a Brāhmaṇa or a Chaṇḍāla by birth; of the kind and merciful Jagannātha no body has any monopoly. The vipras are simply boasting, O King, when they say that he is theirs. Vain men, they say this out of *moha*, sheer ignorance. I can make good my case by quoting at random from the Vedas. Upon this the vipras got furious and cried.:—"Ask him immediately to do this." And at this the king ordered 'Well then maintain your position, O Vaiṣṇava, as you say.' I replied, 'Hear me, O King, You seem to have been highly annoyed. However, be pleased, O King, to go to the place of our King with the whole troop of your Brāhmaṇas. With the grace of our Lord he will explain by quoting lines from the Vedas and the Vedānta all that you may be pleased to ask of him.' Then the King strengthened himself upon his point as far and as much as he could, and triumphantly went there. In the meanwhile the viṣayī (adviser) went and informed chhāmu-karaṇa (private secretary) of what had happened. But afraid to go back home, I remained at the foot of the banian tree. At dead of night Narahari smiled pleasantly and said merrily, 'I do always dwell in the heart of the *great lotus* (*sahasra-dala-padma*). Not aware of this the king and the Brāhmaṇas quarrel with my votaries. (But they should know that) my votary is my life (so to speak).' Saying this He went away. The next morning the king remembered (my challenge) and came (to my place) with the vipras. Dull and ignorant from birth and fond of quarrel-ing, the king was very angry and quarrelled with the votaries. He had a çūdra brought before him and ordered him again to explain the Vedas. Upon this I became all of a sudden unconscious of my body, *i.e.*, became absorbed in a trance and lived in the soul. And thus I thought within myself, 'I have been slighted before the king. The vipras about him have laughed me to scorn. Murāri, the destroyer of all fears and dreads—O Narahari, do come to me. I do beseech Thee.' And when I was thus praying within myself, I heard the reassuring voice of Hari Dāmo-dara, dotingly fond of his votaries—standing before me in a vision out of pity and kindness. Then thus reassured, and concentrating my mind upon the thought of Çrī Hari, I said "Hear me, O best of Kings, it is no fault of ours then that you want to hear the principles of the Vedas from the lips of a Çūdra. If you do this, you will lose in virtue. This Jaḍa is dumb and ignorant and maintains himself by begging alms in Kṣetra. You yourself know this and will not therefore, I pray, be offended at what I say.' But Kṛṣṇa whispered Sārasvata knowledge in the ears of Jaḍa and I placed my hand upon his head. He looked up and smiled. The Vipras said, 'If he can say this, we shall acknowledge ourselves defeated by a dāsa (çūdra).' Hearing this my indwelling spirit got enraged and called aloud, 'Be pleased, my friend Jaḍa, to say your say.' Then Jaḍa said 'Hear me, O king, I shall clearly tell you the details of creation. From the *Nitya*, the Eternal and Absolute, sprang Çūnya into existence, out of which came Praṇava. From this Praṇava again did Çabda, come out and from the Çabdas the Vedas were developed; and from these again the whole creation came into being. This is what we learn from the Vedānta." At this the king and all the vipras present were completely taken aback. After a pause the king said out of great delight, 'Hear me O Dāsa. Siddhi is certainly within your reach. You are no doubt a very great man blessed in the possession of all knowledge. It cannot be that this çūdra has said all this; (he must have done so under an inspiration from you) who are the master of all secrets. Be pleased to delight me by pouring into my ears the honey of *Bhedajnāna*, (knowledge arising out of the consciousness of difference). This çūdra Jaḍa is a great dullard. He can never speak of the beauties of the Vedas; otherwise these will be disgraced and lowered in the estimation of the public. You are a well-informed and wise man. Please explain to me the beauties of the Vedānta." I was much pleased to hear the words of the king and thus prayed "O Chakradhara, O Dāmodara, you who are so fond of your votaries, and who are the overthrower of the proud and the vain-glorious, and the extirpator of demons, you have saved me in this crisis. Be pleased again to help me up so that I may so successfully explain the essential principles of the Vedānta before the vipras that the king will be highly pleased to hear me." My mind was then filled with delight at the idea that with the kind favour of my Lord I shall be able to disperse the cloud of doubt that had gathered over the minds of the vipras; and it was soon concentrated upon the thought of the Lord. Then slowly but steadily He became visible before my mental eyes and the Bhedajñāna, in the form of a dialogue between Çrī Kṛṣṇa and Arjuna, illumed the recesses of my mind. And this instruction delivered in response to the request of Çrī Sāmanta Deva, which I learnt from the lips, as it were, of the Creator, is the honeyed essence of the Praṇava Gupta-Gītā of this humble Balaram Dāsa (*i.e.*, my humble self)."[1]

---

[1] "मुकति-मण्डप परे विप्र । वेदान्तशास्त्र गीता गोप्य ॥ ५
विचार शुणिलि सभीरे । प्रणवगीतार विचारे ॥ ६
तहिं देखिले विप्र मोते । धिकारे गालि देले जेते ॥ ७
केते कहिबि ताङ्क गालि । राजाङ्क आगे मो गुहारि ॥ ८
प्रतापरुद्र महाराजा । कोपे बोइले बड़ पर्य्या ॥ ९
प्रणव वेदवादमान । कि अधिकारि शूद्रज्ञान ॥ १०

From Balarāma Dāsa's account of himself we learn that it was during the reign of Rājā Pratāparudra Deva that he first came into prominence. For some time he was held in esteem and treated with consideration by this king, though afterwards for certain reasons

---

एमन्त उचित नो हइ। ता शुणि हसिलइं मुइ॥ ११
शुण हे नृप गजपति। काहारि नोहन्ति श्रीपति॥ १२
भक्त जनङ्कर से हरि। विप्र चाण्डाल से आदि करि॥ १३
करुणामय जगन्नाथ। काहारि नोहन्ति एकत॥ १४
विप्र जे बोलन्ति आम्भर। गर्ब्ब करन्ति नृपवर॥ १५
मोह बोइल तुच्छ जन। वेद कहिब अनुचण॥ १६
शुणि क्रोधरे विप्रगणे। ए कहुं वेद इहा खने॥ १७
शुणि नृपति काष्टा कला। कह हे वैष्णव बइला॥ १८
आम्भे बोइलु शुण नृप। तुम्भे त कल बड़ कोप॥ १९
कालि प्रभात विप्रगण। नृपति थिबहे आपण॥ २०
जाहा विचारि पचारिब। मूक राजाकु सेलागिब॥ २१
वेदवेदान्त से कहिब। श्रीहरि कृपाए हइब॥ २२
शुणि राजन हड़ कला। विस्मय करि तहुं गला॥ २३
एमन्ते बड अवकाशे। क्षामुरे जनाइले विश्वं॥ २४
बटमूलरे मु रहिलि। सभये घरकु न गलि॥ २५
महानिशारे नरहरि। हसि कहन्ति ठंकरि॥ २६
वर कमल वेनि स्थाने। थिबइ मुइ अनुखने॥ २७
विप्रे नृपति न जानन्ति। भक्तकु विवाद करन्ति॥ २८
भक्त मोहर निज प्राण। कहि चलिले नारायण॥ २९
प्रभाते राजा सभे थिला। विप्रङ्क वेनि चलिगला॥ ३०
क्रोध करिण नरपति। भक्तकु विवाद करन्ति॥ ३१
विवाद मनरे नृपति। जन्मरु मूर्ख जड़मति॥ २२
आणिला एक शूद्र जन। बोइला कह वेद पुण॥ ३३
ता शुणि साहसा मोहर। अज्ञान छाड़िला शरीर॥ ३४
मने विचार कलि मुइ। लघु छाड़िलि राजा ठाइ॥ ३५

he had to retire from the stage of the Court and pass his days in disguise and concealment.

Twenty two years after the death of Pratāparudra and at the accession of Mukunda Deva in 1551 A.D. the political firmament of Utkala began to be convulsed with stupendous changes. Mukunda Deva was a zealous supporter of the cause of Buddhism. Under his auspices Balarāma Dāsa re-entered the arena of religion which he had

---

विप्रे चळन्ति राजा पाश। करिले हास परिहास ॥ ३६
आतङ्कनाशन मुरारि। डाकिलि आन नरहरि ॥ ३७
तहिँहि विचारइ मने। हरि जे कहिले स्वपने ॥ ३८
भक्तवत्सल दामोदर। करुणा करि ए ठार ॥ ३९
एनु भरसा कलि मन। श्रीहरि हृदे कलि ध्यान ॥ ४०
बोलइ शुण नृपवर। नाहिटि दोष हे मोहर ॥ ४१
शूद्रमुखरु वेदवाणी। तुम्भे शुणिव जेबे पुणि ॥ ४२
मूर्ख मोन जडा एहि। सेतमन्त्र मागि खाइ ॥
ताहात जान नृपवर। ए मोर दोष हे न धर ॥ ४४
कथा बोलिण तार कर्णे। बोइला सारस्वत ज्ञाने ॥४५
शिररे कर देलि मुइ। हसिला जडामुख चाहि ॥ ४६
विप्र बोइले ए कहिव। दासेहे निलज होइव ॥ ४७
ता शुणि क्रोध मोर देही। डाकिलि कह जडा भाइ ॥ ४८
जडा बोलइ शुण राजा। निगम आश्रिवि सृष्टि सर्ज्जा ॥ ४९
नित्यरु शून्य होए जात। शून्यरु प्रणव सम्भूत ॥ ५०
प्रणव शवद जनमिला। शवदु वेद य होइला ॥ ५१
वेदु सकल सृष्टि होइ। एमन्ते वेदान्त वुलाइ ॥ ५२
ता शुणि राजा विप्रगण। चकिते न फुरे वचन ॥ ५३
बोइलि नृपति आनन्दे। शुण हे दासे सिद्धि साध्ये ॥ ५४
तुम्भे महत वड लोक। जान सकल ज्ञानसुख ॥ ५५
ए शूद्र न कह ए वाणी। तुम्भे सकल परिमाणी ॥ ५६
कह भेद ज्ञानरस। शुणि ता होइवु सन्तोष ॥ ५७

left during the latter part of the reign of Pratāparudra. And this has probably been represented as his second birth. From the following extract we get a faint glimpse into the political condition of Utkala during the reign of Rājā Pratāparudra:—

"A very curious anecdote is related of his conduct, which seems to show that the followers of Buddha continued to form a sect of importance in this part of India until the beginning of the sixteenth century. It is said that a serious robbery happened in the Rājā's palace, and that he (Pratāparudra) being anxious to discover the perpetrators, assembled together all the wise men, both of the Buddhist and the Brahminical

---

शूद्र पाषण्ड मूर्ख जड़ा । एहु न कहु वेदलीला ॥ ५८
बेदकु निन्दिन हइव । जनरें विक्षत सुभिव ॥ ५९
विप्रङ्क करि नमस्कार । भासा प्रकृतरे विचार ॥ ६०
तुम्भे त सुविज्ञ पुरुष । कह वेदान्त विद्यारस ॥ ६१
शुणि राजनर वचन । शुणि सन्तोष हला मन ॥ ६२
बोलइ शुण चक्रधर । भक्तवत्सल दामोदर ॥ ६३
गर्व्वगञ्जन दैत्यारि । तारिखु ए सङ्कटु हरि ॥ ६४
एवे करुणा कर मोते । कहिवि विप्रङ्क चयते ॥ ६५
शुणि नृपति हेव तोष । वेदान्तसारज्ञानरस ॥ ६६
विप्रङ्क सन्देह फिटिव । मोते करुणा प्रभु हेव ॥ ६७
एते सनाइ मो आनन्द । मने पिञ्जिल पद्मपाद ॥ ६८
तत्‌चखे पद मो मनरे । प्रवेश होइला सधीरें ॥ ६९
श्रीकृष्ण अर्ज्जुन संवाद । मनि प्रवेश हला भेद ॥ ७०
श्रीसामन्तदेव संवाद । जा कहिले पद्मपाद ॥ ७१
कहए बलराम दास । प्रणव गुप्तगीतारस ॥ ७२

(प्रणवगीता १म अ:)

persuasion, to obtain their assistance in prosecuting an investigation. The Brahmins could tell nothing, but the followers of Buddha, through their knowledge of the occult art, were enabled to point out both the offender and the place where the stolen property was concealed. The Rājā was induced by this incident to form so high an opinion of the learning and skill of the Buddhists, that he became for some time a warm supporter of that sect. His Rāṇī, on the other hand, espoused zealously the cause of the Brāhmins. It was at last determined to make another formal trial of their relative skill as men of science and magicians. Accordingly a snake was secretly put into an earthen jar, the mouth of which being covered up, the vessel was produced in a great assembly at the palace. Both parties were then asked what the jar contained. The Brahmins answered,—" It contains only earth;" and sure enough, when opened it was found to contain nothing but earth. This specimen of skill entirely changed the Rājā's opinions, but he now became as violent against the Buddhists as he had been before prejudiced in their favour—so much so that he not only withdrew his protection and countenance, but violently expelled the whole sect from his dominions, and destroyed all their books. It is added that about this time Chaitanya Mahāprabhu came from Nadia in Bengal to visit the temple of Jagannātha, and that he performed miracles before the Rājā".*

* Sterling's *Orissa*, (Edition of 1904) pp. 80—81.

Though the Buddhists were persecuted during the time of Pratāparudra Deva, yet they succeeded, as we learn from other sources, in securing largely the patronage of Rājā Telaŋga Mukunda Deva. Thus the Tibetan work Pogsom says—"Mukunda Deva (Dharma Rāja), king of Otivisa (Orissa) who favoured Buddhism, became powerful. His power extended up to Magadha. He, too, did some service to the cause of Buddhism."

Indeed we may, on the authority of Praṇava Gītā, make bold to assert that although Balarāma Dāsa generally passed for a Vaiṣṇava, yet he was, while in the court of Pratāparudra Deva, but a staunch champion of the doctrine of Çūnya as inculcated by the Mādhyamika philosophy.

From the contemporary events of the times of Rājā Pratāparudra we glean that jealousies of the Brāhmaṇa-Paṇḍits and persecutions by the king soon turned the court into a bed of thorns for Balarāma Dāsa who, in consequence, retired not only from it, but from society altogether. This swelling tide of persecution soon drove the Bāthuris or Bāuris and other kindred tribes into dense jungles and tractless forests. This point has, however, been already dealt with at some length in connection with our treatment of the Bāthuri tribe; so we content ourselves here with only a passing reference. It will now, we hope, become clear after our repeated quotations from the writings of Balarāma Dāsa, that the sole burden of his religious and poetical effusions was the doctrine of the Great Void, as promulgated by Nāgārjuna and forming the nucleus of the Mādhyamika philosophy. In his works on Advaita philosophy Çankara tried to refute the doctrine of Çūnya and to establish in its place that of Brahman ; while Balarāma Dāsa, though largely borrowing from the Vedānta, went against the Advaitavādins and advocated the cause of the Great Void. Now, we presume on the strength of these facts we may justly assert that Balarāma Dāsa was really a veiled follower of Buddhism, or a Vaiṣṇava-Buddhist.

In the last chapter of his Gupta Gītā, Balarāma Dāsa discloses the centra regulated his whole life—although apparent in every line of his writings, if one would but look for it. Thus he says :—

"Again Arjuna asked Vāsudeva to tell him the particulars about the Gupta Gītā, as there were some who thought that it would again be published in the world, (1). Çrī Hari replied "Hear then O Arjuna—In the twenty-seventh aṇka of king Mukuṇḍa Deva, there will live a man named Çani Paṭanāyaka (2-3). The servant of the meek and humble will call on him and blessing him will sit by his side (4). Seeing him carry the Gupta Gītā under his armpit, Paṭanāyaka will address him thus (5). 'What book is there under your armpit and why do you travel about with it ? (6). We are anxious to learn the truths that are discussed in it. So be pleased, Ye Dāsa, to tell us these wise instructions.' (7). Dāsa said, "It is Gupta-Gītā.—Listen to me, if you are curious." (8). He will just open the book, write Oṁ, touch it with his hand and placing under it a circle or Çūnya-maṇḍala, explain to him its meaning (9-10). as consisting of the three letters अ,उ and म with हं, स and ल (11). The ṣaṭchakras (the six mystic circles) are placed in the Om; and inside that are the fourteen worlds. (12). When he will learn thus far of the Gītā, his curiosity and eagerness will much increase; (13). and he will ask "Is there anything beyond this? Be pleased to tell me again—I want to know something more. (14). This Gītā, so highly pleasant and interesting, is a sealed book. So I am anxious to hear it from your lips." (15) Hearing him thus, Dāsa will delight his soul by saying, (16). 'It was I myself who wrote this Gītā in the previous birth. But then only the first chapter was done. (17). I shall, however, go on telling you the whole Gītā now. So be all attention.' (18). Upon these words, I thought within myself, highly pleased with his great devotion, "I shall enter his heart and inspire him with the knowledge of the Gītā. (20). Balarāma Dāsa will give that out in words; and (the book thus composed) will be complete in thirty-five chapters." (21). But including the previous one, Balarām Dāsa dealt exhaustively with it in thirty-six chapters. (22). Hearing him Çani Paṭnāyaka, with his three sons, worshipped him and became his disciples." (23). (Gupta Gītā, Chap. 36.)[1]

---

[1] "पुछि अर्ज्जुन वासुदेवे पुछइ गुपत कल विचार।
केंछ भावे पुन: गुपतगीता जे संसारे हेब प्रचार॥ १
श्रीहरि बोइले शुण अर्ज्जुन। मुकुन्ददेव बलि राजन॥ २
सेहि राजार सतादस अङ्के। वैबर्त्ता शनि पटनायके॥ ४

After this there can be no room for doubt that Balarāma Dāsa had, as his mystic symbol, the words, "Om, Çūnya maṇḍalāya namah" (Om, adoration to the great circular void). Gaṇeça-vibhūti is the name of his another work. In an old commentary on it, entitled *Siddhānta-dambara*, by the author himself, the mystic symbol is given in the words "Oṁ Çūnya Brahmaṇe namah" (Om, adoration to the formless Brahman). Although differently expressed, the two symbols

---

ताहांकु भेटिब दीनङ्क दासे । कल्याण करिब वसिब पासे ॥ ४
गुपतगीता अध्या थिव काखे । ताङ्कु पचारिवे पटनाएके ॥ ५
कि पुस्तक दासे अछि काखरे । फेड़ि पुथि दासे कहथि थरे ॥ ६
आम्भे शुण किना कि कि रहस । दासे बोइले ज्ञान उपदेश ॥ ७
गुपतगीता अध्याय अटइ । गीता नवे हेब शुण कहइ ॥ ८
प्रथमे पुथि फेड़िण कहिवे । ओङ्कार थापि हात मारि देवे ॥ ९
शून्यमण्डलाय ताहाले देइ । ताहाकु दासे कहिबे भेदाइ ॥ १०
अकार उकार मकार तिनि । हंकार सकार लकार घेनि ॥ ११
ओङ्कार मध्ये षड़चक्र स्थान । तथि भितरे चौद्द भुवन ॥ १२
से गीता अध्याक शुणिला जहुं । अवधा माड़्र वाड़िला तहुं ॥ १३
एतिकि गीता कि अधिक अछि । फेड़ कह किमा शुणिवा किछि ॥ १४
ए ये गुपत महारसगीता । आपन कह हइण श्रोता ॥ १५
ताहाङ्क वचन शुणिण दासे । प्रश्न करिवे ता भाव आसे ॥ १६
पूर्ब्ब जन्म आम्भ ए गीता वाला । प्रथम अध्यासिना होइथिला ॥ १७
एवे आम्भे गीता कहिबा रहि । तुम्भे शुण किना श्रवण देइ ॥ १८
से पुथि मोर छामुरे जणाइ । अनेक भक्तिरे प्रसन्न होइ ॥ १९
सु तार हृदये पशिवि जाइ । गीता ताहाङ्कु देउथिवि कहि ॥ २०
तेण कहिव वलराम दास । पञ्चतिश अध्या हइब शेष ॥ २१
पूर्ब्ब अध्या घेनि छत्तिश सरि । बलराम दास कहे बिस्तारि ॥ २२
शुणिण मणि पठनायक । तिन पुत घेनि करि सेवक ॥"

(गुप्तगीता ३६ अध्याय ।)

refer but to one and the same thing. And it goes without saying that the idea underlying these mystic symbols is also the cardinal doctrine of the Mahāyāna Buddhists.

Similarly, Achyutānanda was also a follower of esoteric Buddhism, though openly professing Vaiṣṇavism. Thus, in spite of his profession as a follower of Çrī Chaitanya and disciple of Sanātana Gosvāmin, he incurred the severe displeasure and open hostility of the Brāhmaṇa Paṇḍitas of the court of Rājā Pratāparudra for his openly upholding the doctrine of the Çūnya before that very monarch. To this he thus refers in his Çūnya Saṁhitā.—

"Pratāparudra Deva urged me strongly, and pressure was also brought to bear upon me in the temple. I was asked 'Hear me, O Dāsa, tell me from what *mantra* your *bhajana-mantra* is derived. Of Anāma (the nameless), Nāma (the name), the Kāmavījas, and the revolving in mind of the twenty-four-worded Gāyatrī, tell me which one is your favourite; and furnish me, O Dāsa, with a clear exposition thereof.' The ingenious arguments put forward by the Brāhmaṇas, though fallacious, made the king dubious in mind. He added, 'The Brāhmaṇas are known to be well acquainted with the mantras. They are supposed to possess Brahmajñāna and to know the mantras and the rules laid down in the Çāstras. These Brāhmaṇas have urged me strongly to ask you to explain without delay, and clearly and lucidly, the worship of the Çūnya.' Then, there, in a clearly visible place, I put down the thirty-two letters in the following manner. Nāma was placed under the Anāma, and thus was Kāmavīja written. The five classes (of consonants) and the twelve mātrās were placed; and also the *yantra* was drawn and placed there. Having seen this the Brāhmaṇas were thunderstruck, and said 'Yes, Dāsa, you know the real truth and the underlying import of things. The knowledge of truth and reality is very abstruse and mysterious. Therefore do speak to us of *tattva* clearly and lucidly. You have indeed placed very mysterious words before us, writing Anāma, Nāma and the Kāmavījas and Om in a descending series. This is strange and has never been observed before, and is in reality such as has never been mentioned in the Purāṇas. Where have you learnt this, O Dāsa, and who are they that worship according to this? And who is there that worship Nāma? Conversant with all these *tattvas*, as you seem to be, be pleased to explain this to us.' Thus the Brāhmaṇas did urge me very strongly. The king also again said to me 'Hear me, O Dāsa, You have drawn the *yantra*. Now be pleased to tell us the *mantra*, and the manner in which you perform your worship with that mantra. Furnish me (in short) with a clear exposition of all these.' Hearing again this peremptory request of the king, I felt rather distressed in mind and said 'Hear then O King, my *mantra* is *nirākāra* and I worship the Çūnya. Āsanaçuddhi (purification of the seat) and Aŋganyāsa (the touching of certain parts of the body as enjoined by the Çāstras) are not needed, nor have Sthānabhaŋga and Dikbandhana to be observed. One has to sit in Çūnya and worship, to destroy death and go to Golaka (the place of eternal bliss). The subject of this worship is only Nāma. Because, where is there anything beyond it? Then 'What does this Dāsa say?' saying this the Brāhmaṇas sprang up and prepared to go away. They said further 'Let the king have a test of how the worship of the Çūnya is to be performed. Even here this Dāsa must submit to this examination.' Again one of the Brāhmaṇas smiled and said 'Let him be dropped down into the waters of a well and let's see how he draws his *yantra* there and worships his Çūnya.' Thus confusion and disorder reigned there. The king forgot all about the *mantra* and was carried away by the desire for examining me. When thus confusion and disorder prevailed, the God of the ocean of mercy took compassion on me. The Brāhmaṇas set up a loud uproar and none cared to examine my *mantra*. Knowing that if what the Lord has made a secret of, were to be revealed by the king, there would be no end of the terrible difficulties and dangers that would beset him, my mind was rather set at rest by this confusion. But the Great Lord who is the healer of all troubled hearts again spread a confusion (amonst the Brāhmaṇas). At this time when there was a loud clamour, the king took me by the hand and went away to the widest street. Even here the crowd mustered so strong that there was a loud uproar arising from the people elbowing one another.

"The king said 'Now commence your worship just here near the empty well at Bānkimuhānā. Let these Brāhmaṇas see you submit to an examination of your secret worship before us.' Upon this I was greatly afraid in mind. I then drew my mind away from the numberless people around me, placed the thirty-two letters upon my heart and sitting straight up from the navel became absorbed in meditation. Then with upturned face, I annihilated the mind and concentrated myself upon the idea of the Nirākāra. Having thus lifted life up, I was soon sitting in the void and lost in the idea of Paramahaṁsa. The king was startled to see this and the Brāhmaṇas were thunderstruck. They were pondering in silence—who it is that has thus revealed the unrevealed !—Having seen all this the king became convinced, and mildly and sweetly said "Come, come, Dāsa." He then embraced me and I was pleased to hear these reassuring words, 'Hear me, Achyuta Dāsa. Go and live near Bāṇkimuhāṇā. It is because the name of Achyuta or Inseparable was not disgraced that the worship of Nirākāra Çūnya was made possible. Certainly it is a deep mystery and the manner in which you have explained it has much pleased me.' The king then went away from there, and the Brāhmaṇas thus greatly mortified and humiliated could say nothing. Thus we five* came out of the great and difficult ordeal we were made to undergo and we got a good and secluded place where we plunged into the meditation of Çūnya."[1]

---

* The five are Achyuta Dāsa, Balarāma Dāsa, Jagannātha Dāsa, Yaçovanta Dāsa and Ananta Dāsa.

[1] "प्रतापरुद्र देव कटालिला । देखन्त बहुत प्राकट हेला ॥
बोइले दासे शुण मोह ठारु । भजनमन्त्र कैउं मन्त्र ठारु ॥

The doctrines of the Çūnyavāda as discussed above are akin to those which obtain amongst the Buddhists of Nepal even now. The nature and meaning of the "Great Void" will be understood from the explanation given by Mr. Hodgson on the authority of the Buddhistic scriptures of Nepal:—

"Mahā-Çūnyatā is, according to some, Svabhāva and according to others Içvara. It is

---

अनाम नाम कामवीजमान । गाइवी अब्धि अक्षर भजन ॥
कोउ' मन्त्र गोढ़ि इष्ट तुम्भर । कह देखि दासे तत्त्व विचार ॥
ब्राह्मणे अति चलाइ कहिले । राजन मनकु चञ्चल कले ॥
थोके ब्राह्मणे मन्त्ररे प्रसिद्धि । जानन्ति ब्रह्मज्ञान-मन्त्र-विधि ॥
बहुत कटाक्ष कले मो ठारे । अच्युतदासे कह हे सत्वरे ॥
साक्षाते प्राये मोते कहि देले । शून्यभजन कहतु बोइले ॥
से ठारु हुअइ हेले मते येनु । द्वात्रिंशाक्षर स्थापिलि मु तेणु ॥
अनामतलें नामकु देइण । कामवीज ओमिति कि लखिण ॥
पञ्चवर्ण वार मावा देइण । यन्त्ररे लेखि करिनु स्थापन ॥
देखि ब्राह्मणे हेले आचम्बित । बोइले दास जाण तत्त्व अर्थ ॥
बेल बेल दास कहइ तत्त्व । तत्त्वबोध दास अति गुपत ॥
गहण कथा स्थापिलात तुम्भे । कह दासे देखि शुणिमा आम्भे ॥
अनाम नाम कामवीजमान । ओंकार स्थापि तहिं तले पुण ॥
एत असम्भव अलख्य कथा । पुराण ग्रन्थे शुणिवाइं यथा ॥
काहुं शिखिलं दासे इहा पुणि । एहाकु कोंउ' भजनरे पुणि ॥
कोंउ' भजन अटे नामर ॥ तत्त्व बोधा दासे कह निकर ॥
बहुत कटाक्ष ब्राह्मणे कल । राजन कामुरे पुणि कहिले ॥
राजन बोइले शुण हे दासे । यन्त्र स्थापिल मन्त्र कह तोषे ॥
किरूपे ए मन्त्र भजन कर । कह दासे देखि एथि विचार ॥
पुणि शुणि राजा कटाक्ष कला । शुणि मो मने सङ्कट पड़िला ॥
बोइलि तुम्भे शुण हे राजन । मन्त्र निराकार शून्यभजन ॥

like the ethereal expanse, and self-sustained. In that Mahā-Çūnyatā, the letter A, with the Vīja Mantra of Upāya and the chief of all the Vīja Mantras of the letters, became manifest."

(Rakṣābhagavatī.)

"He whose image is Çūnaytā, who is like a cypher or point, infinite, unsustained (in Nivṛtti),

---

आसनशुद्धि अङ्गन्यास नाहिं ।	स्थानभङ्ग दिक्‌बन्धन नाहिं
शून्यरे वसि भजन करिब ।	कालकु नाशि गोलकरे ठाव ॥
ए भजन नाम अटइ एहि ।	एथुं अधिक आउ पुन काहिं ॥
ब्राह्मणे शुणि चालण उठिले ।	दासे कि कहन्ति बलि बोइले ॥
बोइले ये दासे शून्यभजन ।	राजन एहा करन्तु प्रच्छिन्न ॥
शून्यभजन किरुपे करिबे ।	दासे परीक्षा एहि ठारे देबे ॥
एक ब्राह्मण बोइलेक हसि ।	कूप कि बाम्फि याइण निरसि ॥
देखिबा दासङ्क शून्यभजन ।	किरुपे यन्त्रकु कले स्थापन ॥
एमन्ते कहन्ते धन्दोल हेला ।	मन्त्र छाड़ि राजा परीक्षे भोला ॥
गोल धन्दोल एमन्ते लागिला ।	कृपा-जल-निधि करुणा थिला ॥
गोलरे ब्राह्मणे मालि रहिले ।	मन्त्र प्रच्छिन्न केहिणे करिले ॥
से ठाव मन छोइला उसत ।	जानिलि प्रभु कलित गुपत ॥
राजन येबे प्रच्छिन्न करन्ता ।	विपद आपद माड़ि पड़न्ता ॥
महाप्रभु से आरतभञ्जण ।	आणि धन्दोल लगाइले पुन ॥
एमन्ते प्रहरे गोल लागिला ।	राजन मोते धरि घेणि गला ॥
बड़दाण्डरेत छोइला मोल ।	ठेलाठेलि लोके अति गहल ॥
बाड़िमुहाणि शून्य-बाम्फि ठारे ।	भजन कर दासे एहि ठारे ॥
देखन्तु येतेक ए द्विजवर ।	प्रच्छन्ने परीक्षा आम्भ छामुर ॥
शुणि मो मनरे लागिला भय ।	अनन्त मुरति कलिमु लय ॥
द्वाविंश अक्षर हृदे स्थापिलि ।	नाभि परे बसि ध्यान मुं कलि ॥
ऊर्द्ध मुख करि कलिमु लय ।	निराकार रूप कलिमु ध्याय ॥
प्राण ऊर्द्धं करि शून्ये रहिलि ।	परमहंसे चित्त बुड़ाइलि ॥
देखिण राजन हेले चकित ।	ब्राह्मणे देखि होइला स्थगित ॥

and sustained (in Pravṛtti) whose essence is (Nivṛtti), of whom all things are forms (in Pravṛtti), who is the Īçvara, the first intellectual essence, the Ādi Buddha, was revealed by his own will. This self-existent is he whom all know as the true Being; and, though the state of Nivṛtti be his proper and enduring state, yet for the sake of Pravṛitti (creation), having become Pancha-jñānātmikā, he produced the five Buddhas thus:—from Suviçuddha-dharmadhātuja-jñāna, Vairochana, the supremely wise, from whom proceed the element of Ākāsa, the organ of sight and colours; and from Adarcana-jñāna, Akṣobhya, from whom proceed the element of air, the organ of hearing and all sound; and from Pratyavekṣaṇa-jñāna, Ratna-sambhava, from whom proceed the element of fire, the organ of smell, and all odours; and fron ̣āntajñāna, Amitābha, from whom proceed the element of water, the organ of taste and all savours; and from Kṛtyanuṣṭha-jñāna, Amoghasiddha, from whom proceed the element of earth, the organ of touch, and all the sensible properties of outward things dependent thereon.

थोक आचम्बित रहिले । गुपत प्रघट केमवा कले ॥
राजन देखिण परते गले । दासे आस वलि आटु कहिले ॥
कोलि करिण करे आलिङ्गन । कहि तोषिले आश्वास वचन ॥
गुण आम्भ वाणी अच्युतदास । वाङ्किमुहाण कर ये निवास ॥
अच्युत नाम च्युत नहे येणु । निराकार शून्यभजन तेणु ॥
अतिहि गुपत अच्युतदास ॥ तत्त्वबोध दास अति हरष ॥
से ठारु राजन चलिनु गले । लाजे ब्राह्मणे किछि न कहिले ॥
एमन्त प्रकारे पञ्चजनकु । कटाक्ष कला ये आम्भमानकु ॥
पकन्न परम स्थानु पाइलु । निरालम्ब ध्याने निमग्न हेलु ॥"

All these five Buddhas are Pravṛtti-karmā-nas, or the authors of creation. And these five Buddhas each produced a Bodhisattva. The five Bodhisattvas are *Sristi-karmānas* or the immediate agents of creation; and each, in his turn having become *Sarvaguna*, produced all things by his fiat." . . .

" Çūnyatā, or the total abstraction of phænomenal properties, is the result of the total suspension of nature's activity. It is the *Ubi*, and the *modus*, of the universal material principal in its proper and enduring state of *nivritti* or of rest. It is not nothingness, except with the sceptical few. The opposite of Çūnyatā is Avidyā, which is the mundane affection of the universal principle, or the universal principle in a state of activity;... in other words, it represents phænomenal entities or the n of phænomena, which are regarded as wholly unreal, and hence their existence is ascribed to ignorance or Avidyā."*

This interpretation holds good equally in the cases of the crypto-Buddhists of Utkal outwardly professing the Vaiṣṇava creed, and of the Buddhist Newars. The theory of the void is identical with that of an all-pervading Brahman as will be seen from the above quotation. Needless to say that this theory belongs to the Mahāyāna school.

* Hodgson's Nepal, p. 74, 75, 77, 105.

FIVE VISNUS OR FIVE DHYANI BUDDHAS

In his Viṣṇu-garbha Chaitanya Dāsa was the first to raise the question—" People in general know only of one Viṣṇu. How then are we to account for the belief in five more?" And then he attempts at a solution of the question, as will be found from the following long extract* :—

" He is an invisible, imperceptible being, devoid of all forms and colours. He has no dwelling place and is in reality the Mahā-Çūnya. 199. Destitute of all forms and colours, his body is all formless, and mixed up with Çūnya he is as good as Çūnya. 200. It was beyond the power of any one to describe his form and colour when he assumed these. Even the Veda-Brahma failed to sing his glories. 201. He was formless and colourless, and even amongst the millions of gods there was none comparable with him. One might search throughout the fourteen universes yet one would not find his equal. 202. Nowhere is his equal to be found—

---

* "अगोचर पुरुष से नाहि रूपवर्ण ।
स्थिति नाहि तार अटे महाशून्य ॥ १९९
रूपवर्ण न होइ से अरूप तार देहि ।
शून्यर सङ्गते से शून्य होइ थाई ॥ २००
देह वर्ण स्वरूप के कहिब रूपवर्ण ।
याहार महिमा बखाणि न पारन्ति वेदब्रह्म ॥ २०१
अरूप अवर्ण से त्रय देवाकु न छिला उपमा ।
चौद्द ब्रह्माण्ड खुंजिले नाहि प्रतिसोभा ॥ २०२

so great is the greatness and glory of Alekha. 203. One and the same with Çūnya, he is himself all Çūnya and Çūnya is his form. And identified with Çūnya, he is pervading all space. 204. Çūnya itself is his dwelling place.' 205. Having heard this from the lips of Çaunaka and others, Sanaka had not yet his doubts settled and asked again, 206. "You have spoken, O great and mighty *muni* (sage), of the omniscient origin of all. But the character you have described before me seems to be enveloped in mystery. 207. You say that Alekha is devoid of all forms and colours, that he has no beginning and no end, and that he is in reality Mahāçūnya. 208. How then were the six Viṣṇus born? Be pleased, O high-minded sage, to explain this to me. 209. Branches, flowers and

---

प्र त तुल्य नाल्या मु न भामिलं कांहि ।
एमन्त महिमा मे भलेखर टंहि ॥ २०३
शून्य सङ्गते से शून्य शून्य शून्यरूपो ।
शून्य सङ्गते मिशि भछि सकलस्थानव्यापो ॥ २०४
शून्य हिंटि ताहार भटइ निज घर ।
शून्यरे थाइसे शून्ये करइ बिहार ॥ २०५
सानकादिङ्कर मुखे शुणिलि ए सनक ।
पुणि संशय चिते पुछा कलिक सनक ॥ २०६
बाइलं महामुनि तुम्भे सर्व्वज्ञ भादिमूल ।
केमन चरित्र आम्भर भागे बखानिल ॥ २०७
बोइल भलेखर नाहि रूपवर्ण ।
भाद्य भन्त नाहि तार भटे महाशून्य ॥ २०८
षड विष्णु कांहिरु होइले उतपति ।
इहा मोते बुझाइ कहिब महामति ॥ २१९

fruits are possible only when the tree has its roots; and it rains only after the clouds have been formed. 210. How then can the tree grow without the seed? This is utterly beyond my comprehension. 211. Even after seeds have been sown, trees do not grow without the help of water; and without friction, no fire can be kindled. 212. Hence your assertion that Alekha has no form has raised doubts in my mind. Be pleased somehow to disperse these. 213. (Though Alekha has no form yet) you say that from his body sprang into existence the six Viṣṇus. Of the glories of one I have just now heard. 214. If I can now hear of the respective duties and functions of the remaining five, the doubts of my mind may be set at rest." 215. Upon these words of Sanaka, the sages headed by Çaunaka replied, "The inexplicable glories and

---

वृक्षरे मूल थिलेसिना डालरे फलि फल ।
मेघ आरम्भिलेसिना वरसइ जल ॥ २१०
वीज विना वृक्ष गे केमन्त हेब जात ।
अनुभव बुद्धिरे नो हुअइ आदि अन्त ॥ २११
वीज बुणि जल बिना अङ्कुर न होइ ।
विना घरषणे कांहि अनल उपजइ ॥ २१२
ए मोहर संशय कथा फेडि मोते कह ।
तुम्भे ये बोइल अलेखर नाहि देह ॥ २१३
देहरु जन्य षड़ विष्णु जनमिले ।
एक विष्णुर महिमा शुणिलु कर्णमूले ॥ २१४
आहुरि पञ्च विष्णु काले कि कि कर्म्म ।
तुम्भ श्रीमुखर शुणि छाड़ु मन भ्रम ॥ २१५

greatnesses of Alekha cannot be (even partially) understood with any extraneous aid. 216. Hear us, O Sanaka ; the question that you have raised touches the origin and the end of the māyā of Alekha—which no one can ever know. 217. No one can fully explain his origin and end. No speaker, no words, can express his plays of pleasure. 218. At his own sweet will and pleasure he makes his greatness manifest, and though formless, reveals himself. 219. If he likes, he can assume many forms ; and, if it pleases his mind, he can create many forms. 220. He plays at pleasure, lives at pleasure and assumes many forms at pleasure. 221. His first and own (real) form is Nirākāra. And from his body the form of Dharma is developed. 222. Then living in

---

सनकवचने ये कहन्ति शौनकादि ।
अलेखर महिमा ए अगम्य प्रतिनिधि ॥ २१६
बोइलइ सनक तुम्भे पचारिल याहा ।
आद्य अन्त कहि नुहे अलेखर माया ॥ २१७
विस्तार करि कहिवाकु नु हे आदि अन्त ।
इच्छा सुखे खेलइ ये नाहि ता वाक्य व्यकत ॥ २१८
इच्छा सुखे ताहार महिमा विपाशइ ।
अरूप होइ करिले स्वरूप प्रकाशइ ॥ १२९
इच्छा होइले से अनेक रूप धरे ।
इच्छा हेल मन तार अनेक रूप करे ॥ २२०
इच्छा सुखे खेलइ से इच्छा सुखे रहे ।
इच्छा हेले अनेक से रूपमान होये ॥ २२१
प्रथमे निराकार स्वरूपक होइ ।
धर्म्म स्वरूप होइ तार अङ्गु प्रकाशइ ॥ २२२

imagination only he begins to create; and then again he diverts himself by assuming the form of the good of the world. 223. Hear, Sanaka, of the glories of Alekha. We shall describe to you the attributes and qualities that qualify him. 224. His body, itself devoid of all colours, developed the six colours of white, yellow, red, orange, and of the waterfall and cloud. And out of these six colours were the six Viṣṇus born. 225 226. One of these Viṣṇus was located by Alekha in the eastern Çūnya, one in the western, one in the southern and one in the northern. 227-228. These four Çūnyas are called four Nirākāras; and in reality these Viṣṇus are located just as described here.

* * * *

Having reached the upper Çūnya he became unconscious in the sleep of Yoga and there did spring

---

कल्पना पुरुष होइ पुणि सृष्टि करै जात ।
शिव स्वरूप होइ पुण खेलइ जगत ॥ २२३
शुणइ सनक तुम्भ अलेख महिमा ।
तुम्भ आगे थुके कहिवाकु गुणसीमा ॥ २२४
अवर्ण अङ्ग तार वर्ण प्रकाशिला ।
श्वेत पीत लोहित कुङ्कम चाविकला ॥ २२५
जलधर निझरक एमन्ते षड़ वर्ण ।
ए षड़ वर्णरु षड़ विष्णु हेला जन्म ॥ २२६
पूर्ब्ब शून्ये एक विष्णुङ्कु थापिले ।
पश्चिम शून्यरे एक विष्णुकु रखिले ॥ २२७
दक्षिण शून्ये लेइ राखिले विष्णु एक ।
उत्तर शून्ये एक विष्णु रखिले अलेख ॥ २२८

from him the Brahmās. 229-230. Having been thus born, these gods created the universe consisting of the twenty-one regions of Alekha and the nine parts of the world. 231.

"Each of these universes was an independent entity and for each of these, one Brahmā with his colleagues was created. 233. Having been born, each set of these gods again created a universe, consisting of the twenty-one regions of Alekha and the nine parts of the world. 234. And thus the Brahmās with their subordinates created three Brahmaṇḍas.

"These are known to none but Alekha. 236. The Alekha Puruṣa is present everywhere, yet

---

चारि शून्य चारि वोलाइ निराकार ।
तत्त्व याहा अनुरूपे कलेत विहार ॥ २२९
उपर शून्ये पहुञ्छिले ये योगनिद्रा गले ।
ताहाङ्कर तहुँ ब्रह्मामाने जात हेले ॥ २३०
जात होइ ब्रह्ममाने रचिले ब्रह्माण्ड ।
एकइश पुर अलेख पृथी नवखण्ड ॥ २३१
देवनाग नर जे आदिखानि लेखा ।
ब्रह्माण्डपालन आदि यमन्त येहि शाखा ॥ २३२
एक ब्रह्माण्डमानङ्कर प्रति प्रति तुले ।
ताहांङ्कर तहुँ ब्रह्मामाने जात हेलि ॥ २३३
जात होइ ब्रह्मामाने रचिले ब्रह्माण्ड ।
एकइश पुर अलेख पृथी नवखण्ड ॥ २३४
एक ब्रह्माण्ड मानङ्कर एक एक तुले ।
से तिन ब्रह्माण्ड ब्रह्मामाने सृष्टि कले ॥ २१५

none knows where and what he is, and where and what he is not. 237. Once upon a time one of the Brahmās boasted, "It was I who created the whole universe." 238. . . . . . Another thought within himself, "It was I who created the world with all the movable and immovable things in it." 242. Again another boasted "It was I and none else that was the creator." And thus the four Brahmās created the four Viṣṇus who are placed in the four worlds of Deva, man and serpent. 245. Upon this Sanaka looked upon the faces of Çaunaka and his companions and said "O my lord, what an impossible thing it is that you have just said to me. 245. I have

---

काहार गोचरे एमान मनभेद नाहि ।
सवङ्करि गोचर एक अलेख जानइ ॥ २३६
अलेख पुरुष ये सबु ठारे ठान्ति ।
ताहार भेदाभेद ये केहि न जानन्ति ॥ २३७
एक ब्रह्मा बोइला मु सृष्टि कलि आत ।
मोहर रचनासिना अटइ जगत ॥ २३८
*   *   *   *
एकब्रह्मा कहिले मने गर्वि ।
चराचर करि मु ये रचिलि धरणी ॥ २४१
पुणि एक ब्रह्मा विचारइ मने ।
मु एणि कर्त्ता मो पुरु आन नहि जने ॥ २४३
एहि रूपे चारि ब्रह्मा चारि विष्णु कले ।
देव नर नाग चारिखान थियाइले ॥ २४४
सनक चाइल शौनकादि मुख चाहि ।
असम्भव कथा मोते कहिला गोसाइ ॥ २४५

heard of the glories of four Çūnyas from your lips. And at the time of creation, you say, four Brahmās were born in the four Çūnyas. 246. But the world knows of only one Brahmā and one Viṣṇu; and this has again been confirmed by the four Vedas. 247. How then do you say that there are four Brahmās who are the four Nirākāras and who, from the four directions of the Çūnya, created the universe? 248. This sounds impossible—so much so that even though I have heard the story with my own ears, yet in my mind I am not yet convinced. 249. I do therefore request you to be so good again as to explain this clearly to me.' Hearing him, Çaunaka and his companions said 250. "Hear, Sanaka, of the illusive tricks of Alekha—of the innumerable colours and forms that he has assumed. 251. The glories of that Alekha are always

---

चारिशून्यर महिमा शुणिलि तुम्भ मुखे ।
चारिशून्य चारिब्रह्मा जन्मिछि सृष्टिकल्प ॥ २४६
एक ब्रह्मा एक विष्णु जानन्ति जगते ।
पुणि लेखा हइला से चारि वेदपथे ॥ २४७
तुम्भे कि प्राय बोइला चारि ब्रह्मा चारि निराकार ।
चारिदिक शून्यरे से रचिले संसार ॥ २४८
एकथा असम्भव लागिला कोमते ।
कर्णरे शुणि मने न जाइ परते ॥ २४९
एहर चरित्र मोते फेड़ि कह सन्धि ॥
सनक वचन शुणि बलन्ति शौनकादि ॥ २५०
शुणत सनकहे अलेखर माया ।
केते कैते रूप अच्छियछि काया ॥ २५१

manifest—know that they have no beginning, no middle, no end. 252. We shall try to tell you as clearly as we can, of the origin and the end of him from whom have the countless Brahmāṇḍas sprung. But none can know fully the majesty and greatness of him who is infinite and indefinable and who is above all similarities and differences. 253-254. The greatness of Alekha as described by the Vedas may be compared to the fish in the ocean. And just as when a stone is thrown down, the ocean only knows how it goes but the fish knows nothing of it, so Brahmā and the other gods know but little of the glory and greatness of Alekha. Brahmā speaks only of what he himself has created. 255-257. Again, Viṣṇu cannot say whence he sprang; and the Vedas do speak only

---

से अलेखर सकल महिमा सन्धान ।
आद्य मध्य अन्त तार नाहि बोलि जान ॥ २५२
अनन्त कोटि ब्रह्माण्ड याहार गर्भजात ।
के सम्भि करि कहिब ताहारि आदि अन्त ॥ २५३
अशेष भाव नाहि याहार भेदाभेद ।
ताहार महिमाकु नाहि काहार भेदाभेद ॥ २५४
वेदर महिमा से जलरे अछि मीन ।
जेन दूर थाए जल पखुर मान तिन ॥ २५५
तेन दूर बरता जानइ जलवर ।
आउ ताहाङ्कु तीनिकि दिशइ अन्धकार ॥ २५६
सेहि रूपे ब्रह्मामाने एकथा जानन्ति ।
ब्रह्मा याहा सृजि थाहि से वारता वर्णन्ति ॥ २५७

of one Brahmā and one Viṣṇu. 258. . . 259; while they speak only an iota of the greatness of Alekha, because they cannot ascertain and measure his glory. 260. * * * * There are many scriptures and many other works on the subject but in none of these is to be found any definition of Alekha. 265. But in the Viṣṇugarbha Purāṇa there is an exhaustive account of his glories and greatnesses, though these have no beginning and no end and are really indefinable. 266. The four Çūnya Nirākāras, assumed forms and from their bodies produced the Brahmās. 267.* * Again Sanaka turned his eyes towards Çaunaka and the rest and said "Would you again be pleased to tell me the doings of Viṣṇu? If

---

पुन बिष्णु न वर्णि कांहिरु अन्म होइ ।
एक ब्रह्मा एक विष्णुर महिमा बेद कहि ॥ २५८
आवर कहि बेद अवतार विष्णुनाम कर गुण ।
सृष्टिर शुभाशुभ जेतेक पाठेन ॥ २५९
अलेखर महिमा पुन किछि किछि कहन्ति ।
निर्णय करि महिमा वखानि न पारन्ति ॥ २६०

* * * *

अनेक शास्त्र ये अनेक ग्रन्थमान ।
ए ये नाहि अलेखर निर्णय वचन ॥ २६५
विष्णुगर्भपुराणे अछि अलेखमहिमा ।
अन्त करि नाहि तार आदि अन्त सीमा ॥ २६६
आकार शून्य चारि निराकार हेला ।
ताहारु अङ्गरु पुन ब्रह्मामान जात केला ॥ २६७

* * * *

I hear it from your lips, my doubts will disappear. 271-272. Be pleased to tell me clearly the natures of the various attributes and qualities that were manifested by him when he laid himself down on water." 273. Çaunaka and others replied, "Hear, O Sanaka, we shall give an account of the greatnesses and glories of the Viṣṇus. 274. The sea of milk is in the east. in the west is the sea of water; and in the south-sea there are other varieties of water 275. Dwelling on the shores of each of the seas, they received, each of them, seven names. 276. They were then divided and separated from one another, each as a whole in itself. Again, however, did they receive the appelation of Sapta Sindhu (seven seas). 277. Then having laid themselves down on the seas, the four Nirākāras became unconscious in the sleep of

---

सनक कहन्ति शौनक मुख चाहि ॥ २७१
अ वार वेनि विष्णुचरित मोते कह।
तब मुख शुणिले फिटिब सन्देह ॥ २७२
कि कि मान सम्पद से केल जलशायी।
ताहार चरित मान कहिव बुझाइ ॥ २७३
शौनकादि बोइले तुम्भे शुणहे सनक।
से विष्णुमानङ्कर महिमा परिवाद ॥ २२४
पूर्ब्बमुखे क्षीर सिन्धु पश्चिमे जलद।
दक्षिण दगुब्रते प्रति जगुभेद ॥ २७५
एक एक सिन्धुकूले कले परिणाम।
तहु करि हेले साताङ्क त सात नाम ॥ २७६
एक एक पराण करि रखिले भाग करि।
पुन नाम रखिले सपत सिन्धु बोलि ॥ २७७

Yoga. 278. Meditating upon the Ātman, they became absorbed in the dhyāna of Alekha, whose form was before their vision. 279. To perform different functions innumerable Viṣṇus were born from the hairs on their bodies. 280. In the upper Çūnya was Viṣṇu placed and given the name of Vaikuṇṭhanātha. 281. One Nirākāra was taken to and located in the Chandra Çūnya; his glories are utterly unknowable. 282. He dwells permanently in the sea of nectar and of him all the Viṣṇus are but emanations." 283.

But, we hope, a little close observation will convince any one that the five extra Viṣṇus referred to here are but indentical with the five Dhyāni-Buddhas spoken of in the Buddhistic Scriptures of Nepal. In this manuscript we are told that in the beginning there was only the Great Void (Mahāçūnya), the five elements being

---

समुद्रमान करि आसनमान कलि ।
चारि निराकार तहि योग निद्रा गलि ॥ २७८
आत्माध्यान करि सेहि अलेख ध्याने रहि ।
नयन अग्रे रूप प्रकाश कराइ ॥ २७९
ताहाङ्कर रोमरु अनेक विष्णुजात ।
कार्य्य अनुरूपे से होयन्ति आत्मजात ॥ २८०
उपर शून्ये एक विष्णुङ्क थापिला ।
बैकुण्ठनाथ बोलि तार नाम देला ॥ २८१
चन्द्र शून्ये नेइ थुइला एक निराकार ।
ताहार महिमा मान अति अगोचर ॥ २८२
अमृत सागरे ताहार नित्य वास ।
ताहाङ्क ठंइ विष्णुमाने होयन्ति प्रकाश ॥" २८३

non-existent; there existed only the formless, attributeless, self-existent Viṣṇu as the primordial cause. He brought the universe into existence, and in course of time a desire to do good to this universe possessed his heart. Though really formless, he did now assume a form and was denominated Dharma. At the instant of his conceiving the desire of creation, five forms *i.e.* beings were produced who were also called Viṣṇus. They were white, blue, yellow, red and green. Thus including Mahāviṣṇu (the primordial cause) there were now six Viṣṇus in all. The subordinate five were placed in charge of the different celestial regions—thus, one in the east, one in the west, one in the north and one in the south, and the remaining one in the upper celestial region, where he became deeply absorbed in Dhyāna. And from his body each of the Viṣṇus, again, produced, in his turn, a Brahmā, and to each of these Brahmās was delegated the power and function of creating the universe. After the subordinate five Viṣṇus had created the Brahmās, they lost themselves in the meditation of the Mahāçūnya. The Viṣṇu who was placed in charge of the upper celestial region was known as the Lord of Vaikuṇṭha.

The description, of creation, as given above by Chaitanya Dāsa, is essentially different from what is found in the Brāhmanic scriptures. The cosmogony discussed in the above text is exactly what has been propounded by the Mahāyāna Buddhists in their religious works. Let us now try to discuss and explain the subject more fully.

In reply to the question 'How and when was the world created?' the Mahāyānists affirm that in the beginning there was nothing but Svayambhū who is self-existent. Him they call Ādi Buddha. In the beginning he created, "for the duration of the present systems of worlds," the Pañcha Dhyāni-Buddhas. This theory of creation is exactly what is to be found in Chaitanya Dāsa's work, 'Viṣṇugarbha.' The worship of Ādi Buddha and of the five Dhyāni Buddhas is still prevalent in Nepal. The following extract from Dr. Oldfield's Sketches from Nipal will throw more light on the subject:—

"The Theistic system of Buddhism teaches that one universal, all powerful, and immaterial spirit has existed from before the commencement of time, and that it will pervade the universe throughout all eternity. This Spirit is God. He is possessed of supreme power, and is endowed with supreme intelligence, and is, therefore, called Ādi Buddha.

* * * * * * * *

"The majority of the Theistic Schools believe that while Ādi Buddha represents supreme intelligence, or mind, there is associated with and forming part of Him, yet at the same time totally distinct form Him, another Being, divine and eternal, who represents *Matter*, and who is the sum of all the active powers of the material universe. This Being or Spirit they call Ādi Dharma or Ādi Prajñā.

"These two divine Principles or Spirits, by their union and joint operation form the One Supreme Being, who not only originated the universe, and has since preserved it, but who, by an act of His will, called into being the celestial deities or Buddhas, as well as the lesser Hindu deities, all of whom are looked upon as emanations, more or less directly derived, from this Supreme Intelligence or Ādi Buddha. He is called sometimes Svayambhū or the Self-Existent."*

"Ādi Buddha is believed ever to be, and ever to have been, in a state of perfect repose. The only active part which he is represented ever to have taken with reference to the universe was the bringing into being, by five separate acts of creation, the five Divine Buddhas, as emanation from Himself. These Buddhas are called "Divine," because they spring direct from Ādi Buddha, and they were brought by him into existence merely as instruments through whose agency he might effect the creation of the universe.

"The five Divine Buddhas are ranked in the order in which they were created, 1st, Vairochana; 2nd, Akṣobhya; 3rd, Ratnasambhava; 4th, Amitābha; 5th, Amoghasiddha. They are looked upon as brothers, and in that sense as all holding exactly the same rank; but Vairochana, as eldest brother, theoretically holds the highest position among them; while Amitābha,

* Dr. Oldfield's Nipal, Vol. II. pp. 89-9 .

the fourth brother,—as father to the Bodhisattva Padmapāni, who is lord of the existing universe,—theoretically receives the greatest amount of worship.

"Each of these Buddhas was empowered by Ādi Buddha to produce a subordinate being or Bodhisattva who stood in relation to the Divine Buddha of son to father, and to whom each Buddha delegated all his divine attributes and powers, and having done so, relapsed, or was reabsorbed into the Great First Cause from which he had originally emanated. They have ever since remained in an eternally quiescent state, and are not believed to take the slightest concern in any mundane affairs."*

"The Divine Bodhisattvas having been brought into being, by the association of the (Divine) Buddhas with their Çaktis, expressly for the creation and government of the universe, they are looked upon as types of the active and creative powers of Nature."†

Reading together and comparing the account given in Viṣṇugarbha, and the Newar Buddhistic version, of creation, we find that the infinite, formless and omniscient Viṣṇu of Chaitanya Dāsa was no other than the Svayambhū or the Ādi Buddha of the Mahāyānist, and the subordinate Viṣṇus or celestial beings, created by Parama Viṣṇu, are but the five Dhyānī Buddhas. Further, the Brahmās produced from their bodies by these

* Oldfield, Vol. II. pp 111-112.
† Do. do. p. 115.

lower Viṣṇus, were in reality and essence but the divine Bodhisattvas. We give below what may be called a geneological table of the Dhyāni-Buddhas and the Bodhisattvas as found in the Buddhistic scriptures of Nepal.

ADI BUDDHA

2 Aksobhya.	3. Ratna Sambhava.	1. Vairochana.	4. Amitābha.	5. Amogha Siddha.
2. Vajrapāni.	3. Ratnapāni.	1. Samanta-bhadra.	Padmapāni.	Viçvapāni.

From the above list it will be clear and evident to all that the subject-matter of Chaitanya Dāsa's work was borrowed from the literature of the Mahāyāna Buddhists. The Divine Bodhisattvas were believed by the Mahāyāna School to have been the active authors of creation. "One by one, in succession, they were appointed as creators and governors of the then existing systems of world;"* three of them have since passed away and the present world is the work of the fourth Bodhisattva Padmapāni.

The Hindus regard Buddha as one of the Avatāras of Viṣṇu—an opinion which is also endorsed by the Buddhists of India. In the 10th century A.D. Kṣemendra, a renowned Kashmirian poet and author of the celebrated work 'Avadānakalpalatā' discussed at length the Mahāyāna Buddhism of the day and went so far

* Dr. Oldfield's Nipal, Vol. II. p. 115.

as to declare Buddha as an Avatāra of Viṣṇu. No wonder therefore that the Vaiṣṇavas of Utkala, who are Buddhists in heart though not so in profession, regard Buddha as Viṣṇu himself and the Bodhisattvas as Brahmās. In the extract from Viṣṇugarbha quoted above we find that the author ascribed to the five subordinate Viṣṇus the following five colours—white, yellow, red, blue and green.

We learn from the literature of the Nepal Buddhists that each of the Dhyāni-Buddhas also had a separate colour assigned to him. We give below a list of the five Dhyāni-Buddhas with their respective colours:—

1. Vairochana ... ... White
2. Akṣobhya ... ... Blue
3. Ratnasambhava ... ... Yellow
4. Amitābha ... ... Red
5. Amoghasiddha ... ... Green

And like the author of Viṣṇugarbha who locates these Viṣṇus in different regions of the universe, Buddhist writers also assign to the Dhyāni-Buddhas different Bhavanas or particular mansions of the universe.

Svayambhū Purāṇa, named after Svayambhū or Ādi Buddha is an important Buddhistic Scripture of Nepal. We find in it a passage which runs thus—Vairochana was placed in the upper celestial region of the universe, Akṣobhya in the east, Ratna Sambhava in the south, Amitābha in the west and Amoghasiddha in the north.[1] In several of the Chaityas of Nepal also, the Dhyāni-Buddhas are assigned the same positions as described here.

DHARMA.

Dharma performs an important part of Buddhism, being the second of the Buddhist Trinity. The religious workers, Rāmāī Paṇḍiṭa, Lāusena, and others, who flourished during the reign of Dharmapāla II in the 11th Century A.D., found that this Dharma had lost much in the estimation of the public, and devoted their lives to re-establishing his glory and lost supremacy; and with this object in view they composed the Çūnya Purāṇa and the several Dharma-maŋgalas. In the course of our survey in Mayūrabhañja, we came across several Oriya Manuscripts dealing with the subject of Dharma. From these Manuscripts we can form some idea of the influence which this cult once exercised upon the minds of the people.

The following account of the origin of Dharma and of the creation of the universe by him is given in the Dharma-Gītā of Mahādeva-dāsa :—

"Whose graceful and majestic person is Çūnya

---

1 "ऊर्द्ध्वं * वैरोचनश्चापि पूर्व्वे अक्षोभ्यमित्यपि ।
दक्षिणे रत्नसम्भवं अमिताभ पश्चिमेऽपि ॥
उत्तरेऽमोघसिद्धिश्च इति पञ्चतथागतम् ।"

(A. Society's Edition. pp. 370—371.)

* 'मध्ये" इति पाठान्तरम् ।

and who is without any appetite or desire; who has no form and who is absolutely indescribable and indefinable. 20.*

* * * *

†"In that receptacle of world is the seat of that Lord; and it is this which is the pure and absolute paradise sought by all. And that world is the void of voids—the great void, created out of millions of worlds. 26-27. There is here no sun, no moon, none of the eight tutelary deities of the directions and neither birth nor death, neither warmth nor cold. And in this state did crores of ages elapse. Hear me, I shall tell you how Dharma was born thereafter. 28-29. After Mahāprabhu had destroyed the sins, the glorious face of Dharma emanated from him. 30. After innumerable *Kalpas* had thus elapsed, did the Lord yawn heavily, and out of that yawn

* "शून्य श्रीअङ्ग याहार शून्य भोग्य वासी ।
न श्रोभे वचन रूप रेख नाहि किछि ॥ २०

† से आधार भुवने से प्रभुङ्क आसन ।
से स्थान सनुङ्क शुद्ध वैकुण्ठभुवन ॥ २६
शून्य शून्य महाशून्य से भुवनस्थान ।
लच जेङ्के महाशून्य होइछि निर्म्माण ॥ २७
नाहि सूर्य्य नाहि चन्द्र अष्ट दिक्पाल ।
नाहि जन्म मृत्यु नाहि तपत शीतल ॥ २८
से आसने केते कोटी युग वहि गला ।
शुण एवे धर्म्मजात येमते होइला ॥ २९
महाप्रभु गुणि गुणि पाप पाषे ध्वंस ।
धर्म्मकु श्रीमुख प्रभु कलिक प्रकाश ॥ ३०

through that glorious mouth was Pavana (wind or space) born. Bowing down his head (at the feet of the Lord) Pavana said 'Wherefore have you brought me into existence? Where shall I go?' The Lord replied 'Pavana, blow away quickly and come back after you have created the universe.' And in obedience to the directions of his father, Pavana went away saying 'I shall come back after I have created the world, as asked by you.' On his way, however, he reflected thus, 'If I were to create the world, I should not be able to return after I have seen the pleasures of it.' So he shrank back from the task of creation, and by practising yoga and dhyāna, begot his son Yuga. 31-36. And he asked Yuga, 'You are to go immediately, and to come back only after you have created the world.' Upon receiving the orders

---

केते कल्पे काले प्रभु हाइर माइले ।
से हाइ श्रीमुखरु पवन जात हेले ॥ ३१
उभा होइ पवन जे बोलइ गोंसाइ ।
कांहि थिवि जात मोते कल कांहि पांइ ॥ ३२
प्रभु बोइले पवन धातिकारे थिबु ।
संसार पृथी सृजिण बाहुड़ि आसिबु ॥ ३३
पिता आज्ञा पाइ से पवन चलि गला ।
आसिबि संसार सृजि बोलि काहि गला ॥ ३४
मने विचारिला यदि संसार सृजिवि ।
देखिण संसारसुख आसि न पारिवि ॥ ३५
ए संसार सृजिवाकु पवन डरिला ।
योगध्यान करि युग पुत्र जात कला ॥ ३६

of his father, Yuga flew away quickly, saying 'I shall return only after I have done your bidding.' But on his way he did thus deliberate, 'If I were to undertake the work of creation, I should not be able to come out after I have seen the pleasures of the world.' So he, too, was greatly afraid to undertake the creation and produced out of his body a son named Nirañjana and said to him 'Go immediately and come back only after you have created the world.' 37-41. Having been thus directed by his father Nirañjana did (in reality) go away but was highly afraid to create the world. 42. He could not thus create this world, but begot out of his own person a son named Nirguṇa; 43. and asked him to go

---

युगकु बोइला एहि चण थिबु ।
संसार पृथी सृजिण बाहुड़ि आसिबु ॥ ३७
पिता आज्ञा युग वेगे चलि गला ।
आसिबि संसार सृजि बोलि कहि गला ॥ ३८
बाटे विचारिला मने संसार सृजिबि ।
देखिण संसार सुख आसि न पारिबि ॥ ३९
युग पृथो सृजिबाकु महाभय कला ।
निरञ्जन बोलि पुत्र देहु जात कला ॥ ४०
बोइला तु निरञ्जन एहि खणि थिबु ।
संसार पृथी सृजिण बाहुड़ि आसिबु ॥ ४१
पिता आज्ञा निरञ्जन चलि गला ।
ए संसार सृजिबाकु महाभय कला ॥ ४२
निरञ्जन ए संसार सृजि न पारिला ।
निर्गुण बोलिण पुत्र देहु जात कला ॥ ४३

away instantly and to return after finishing the task of creation. 44. Nirguṇa, too, failed to create the world but produced from his body his son Guṇa 45 ; and said 'You are immediately to go away my child, and return only after you have created the universe.' 46. With these instructions from his father, Guṇa went away quickly but was highly afraid to undertake the task of creation. 47. He thought within himself 'Were I to create the world, I should not be able to come out of it after I have seen its pleasures.' 48. So Guṇa, too, failed to create the world and (in his turn) brought out of his person a son named Thula (Sthūla) ; 49. and told him to go immediately and come back after he had created the universe. 50. Thula flew away

---

वोइला तु निर्गुण एहि खणि यिबु ।
संसार पृथी सृजिण वाहुड़ि आसिब ॥ ४४
निर्गुण हि ए संसार सृजि न पारिला ।
गुण बोलि करि पुत्र देहु जात कला ॥ ४५
गुणकु बोइला बापु एइ खण यिबु ।
संसार पृथी सृजिण वाहुड़ि आसिबु ॥ ४६
पिता आज्ञा पाइ गुण वेगे चलि गेला ।
ए संसार सृजिवाकु महाभय कला ॥ ४७
मने चिन्तारिला यदि संसार सृजिबि ।
देखिण संसार सुख आसि न पारिबि ॥ ४८
गुण हि संसार सृजि न पारिला ।
ठुल बोलि करि पुत्र देहु जात कला ॥ ४९
ठुलकु बोइले बापु एहि खणे यिबु ।
संसार पृथी सृजिण वाहुड़ि आसिबु ॥ ५०

speedily, having been thus directed by his father, but was greatly afraid to undertake the task. 51. He shrank back from creating the universe in great fear and sat down on his way heaving deep sighs. 52. He was absorved in deep meditation and abstraction, and begot of his own person a son named Dharma ; 53. and said to him 'Go quickly, my child, and come back after having (created and) experienced the pleasures of the world.' 54. 'But you must be very quick in going from and coming back to this place, or else you will be overtaken by *Moha* on your way and will never be able to come back at all.' 55. Unable to disobey the words of his father, Dharma went away saying that he would return as soon as he had done with the creation. 56. But even he was afraid to create the world though he had left his father with the above

---

पिता आज्ञा पाइ ठुल वेगे चलि गला ।
ए संसार सृजिवाकु महाभय कला ॥ ५१
ठुल हि डरिला पृथी सजिवार पाइ ।
वाटरे वसिला डरि निश्वास पकाइ ॥ ५२
महायोगध्यान करि ठुल हि वसिला ।
धर्म्म वोलि एक पुत्र देहु जात कला ॥ ५३
धर्म्म कु वोइला वापु वेगें होइ यिबु ।
संसारभोग भुञ्जिंण वाहुड़ि आसिबु ॥ ५४
आसिबु वेग होइतु एजे ठाकु यिवा ।
मोह होइ पड़ि पथे आसि न पारिवा ॥ ५५
पितार वचन धर्म्म भाङ्गि न पारिला ।
आसिवि संसार सृजि बोलि कहि गला ॥ ५६

words and sat down to think out (some way whereby he could extricate himself). 57. He said to himself 'Father's words are inviolable. Were I to fall back from the task of creation, I should meet with certain destruction. 58. But what an insoluble riddle it is! Even the Ṛṣis, when overtaken by *Moha*, come to destruction. How then am I to create *moha* and yet live safe and secure?' 59. Having thus reflected within himself, Dharma sat down in extreme anxiety and trouble of mind, and his body began to perspire. 60. He then wiped his forehead with his hand and shook off the drops of perspiration upon the ground; and from there a woman sprang up. 61. She was a young lady in full bloom with sweet and gentle smiles (upon her lips) . . . . 62. Having seen her, Dharma was amorously inclined, and he

---

धर्म्म हि से संसार सृजिवाकु डरिला ।
पिता वुलि जाइ धर्म्म भालि न वसिला ॥ ५७
वोइलि धर्म्म पिता आज्ञा भाङ्गि न पारिलि ।
संसार न सृजिलेत निश्चय नाश गलि ॥ ५८
मोह होइ पड़ि ऋषिमाने मोह जान्ति ।
मुइ सृजि मोह जिवि करि एकि भान्ति ॥ ५९
देह गम गम घम त्रिपत्र हइला ।
विचारि मनरे धर्म्म भालि न वसिला ॥ ६०
कपालु झाल पाणि हस्ते फिङ्गि देले ।
से पाणि भूमिरे पड़ि स्त्री जनमिले ॥ ६१
नव युवा होइले भूमिरे पड़ि जाइ ।
हसिलि अलप होइ से धीरे अनाइ ॥ ६२

held in hand the seed that flowed out. 66. Then Dharma let the seed drop there, which fell in three different parts. 71. And out of the seed Brahmā, Viṣṇu and Içvara were born. Dharma was highly pleased to see these three sons. 72. Then he said to Brahmā 'You are to go and create the world;' to Viṣṇu 'You are to destroy the demons'; 73. and to Içvara 'Because you occupy a junior place to Brahmā and Viṣṇu, you are to go and practise abstraction and meditation.' 74. 'I am now going away to where my father is; (but) you, three brothers, are to remain here and create the the world.' 75. Then the goddess said "Having begotten me from your forehead, you are my father. How then am I to live with the sons, leaving their father?" 76. Dharma replied 'Why

---

धर्म्म देवतायें देखि ण अखमाल छोइला
खसिलाक बोज अङ्ग हस्तरे धरिला ॥ ६६
एते वोलि धर्म्म वीज से ठारे ढालिले ।
तिन खण्ड होइ वीज से ठारे पड़िले ॥ ७१
पड़िण से ठारे बीज से ब्रह्मा विष्णु जात ।
तिन पुत्र देखि धर्म्म होइले उषत ॥ ७२
ब्रह्माङ्क बोइले तुम्भे पृथी जात कर ।
विष्णुङ्क वोइले तुम्भे असुरङ्क मार ॥ ७३
ईश्वरङ्क वोइले तु योग कर ध्यान ।
ब्रह्मा विष्णु दुइ भाइ ठारु तु जे सान ॥ ७४
आम्भे जउ अछु जे पिता ठाकु मोर ।
तुम्भे तिन भाइ सृजिव संसार ॥ ७५
देवी वोइले कपालु जात कलु मोते ।
वाप छाड़ि पुत्र सङ्गे रहिवि कि मते ॥ ७६

will you go with me? With all the pleasures of the world, all the people will come to worship you here. 77. Brahmā, Viṣṇu and Hara, my three sons, will create here the play-house of the world. 78. (Though but one) you yourself will be millions in form, as tutelary deities of villages; and every day will you have millions of worship the wide world over.' 79. (Then) he added 'Brahmā will create the world and fill this play-house with great dolls (*i.e.*, beings).' 80 . . . And thus were they begotten of Dharma . . . 91. And thus the mother remained here with her sons and having (thus) created the world Dharma went back to the place of his father.' 92.

From the above account of creation quoted *in extenso* we come clearly to know that both the elements and the attributes sprang into existence from the Supreme Lord of the universe, *viz.*,

---

धर्म्म बोलि मागी सङ्गे किपा जिबु ।
पृथ्वी भोग घेनी सब सेबा तु घेनिबु ॥ ७७
ब्रह्मा विष्णु हर तिनि पुत्र सोदर ।
एखाने सृजिबे संसार खेलघर ॥ ७८
तुम्भे लचे रूप हैब ग्रामश्रीरूपे ।
लचे पूजा पाइब दिनर पृथिबी जाके ॥ ७९
बोइलि धर्म्म ब्रह्म सृजिबे संसार ।
महा पुतली आनि करिते खेल घर ॥ ८०
एमन्त प्रकारे तहुँ धर्म्म जात हेला ।
धर्म्म रखि खेति सृजि संसार छोड़ला ॥ ९१
एमन्ते मा पुत्र घेनि ए ठारे रहिलि ।
संसार सृजिण धर्म्म पिता ठाकु गले ॥ ९२"

Mahāçūnya. In the beginning he was destitute of all attributes; then he came to develop attributes and assumed a material form. Thereafter he manifested himself as Dharma and from the sweat of his brow created a beautiful woman representing the primordial energy of the universe. And from this did Brahmā, Viṣṇu and Maheçvara spring; and to them were made over the charge and the care of the creation.

We meet with a similar description of creation in the Çūnya Purāna of Rāmāi Paṇḍita. First of all, he derives the wind or space, time and the elements from the Mahāçūnya and then from his body, which was Dharma itself, Nirañjana. From the sweat of Nirañjana's brow did the primordial energy spring, from which again did Brahmā, Viṣṇu and Maheçvara have their beings. The reader will now agree with us in thinking, we may hope, that the influence of the Dharma cult as expounded by Rāmāi Paṇḍita is largely reflected in the Dharmagītā of Mahādeva Dāsa. Just as one hears certain classes of the people sing Dharma-Maṇgala in different places of the Rādha country, so one will hear, in some parts of Mayūrabhañja, the tribes known as Pāna, Bāthuris, &c., to sing the Dharmagītā by Mahādeva Dāsa.*

Mahādeva Dāsa has also adopted the same theory of creation as has been promulgated

---

* For Dharma cult, see Bengal Census Report, (1901), Pt. I. p. 204, and Discovery of living Buddhism in Bengal, by M. M. Haraprasād Çāstri.

by the Mahāyāna Buddhism. He has also followed Rāmāi Paṇḍita by representing Dharma as male, while the Buddhists of Nepal worship Dharma as a female divinity, giving it the name of Prajñā or the primordial energy.

Balarāma Dāsa also, while designating 'Mahāçūnya' as 'Nirañjana,' regarded 'Dharma' as the primordial energy. Thus in his Gaṇeça-Vibhūti-ṭīkā he says—

"मह्रा नित्यस्थान रेटी ए व्रत प्रमाण ।
आदिमाता देवी से देवता महाशून्य ॥
सखि तंहि आदिमाता सखा निरञ्जन ।
तत्त्व करि कहि देवा हेतु करि चिन ।" । (२य अध्याय)

* * * * *

"That goddess is the Ādimātā and that god is Mahāçūnya. And that Ādimātā and Nirañjana are related to one another as friend. This is the (real) secret, but try to understand them more particularly.'

In the Svayambhū Purāṇa of Nepal Dharma is represented as Prajñā-Pāramitā or Buddha-Mātā *i.e.* the mother of all Buddhas, who has no beginning, no end—

"धर्म्मदयास्वरूपेण त्रैलोक्यं च प्रख्यापिता ।
सर्व्वतथागतानाञ्च जननी इति ख्यापिता ।
खगाननेति नामेन खत्रयंशून्यरूपिणी ॥
शून्यतां शून्यतां माता बुद्धमाता प्रकीर्त्तिता ।
प्रज्ञापारमितारूपी बौद्धानां जननी तथा ।"*

* *Vide* Brihat Svayambhu Purāna (A. Society's Edition), pp. 1-9-18^.

"Dharma is known throughout the three worlds as Dayā (mercy); and is regarded as the mother of all the Tathāgatas. And having the colour of the sky and the form of the Çūnya, she is named Khagānanā.

"Mother Çūnyatā is known as Buddha-Mātā and in the form of Prajñā Pāramitā she is also the mother of the Buddhists."

Just as here Çūnyatā or Prajñā Pāramitā is looked upon as the mother of all the Tathāgatas or Buddhas i.e. as the Ādimātā, so in various places of the Çūnya-Saṁhitā of Achyutānanda, Dharma, or for the matter of that, the void itself, is treated as the mother of all the gods; and the Paramātman is used synonymously with the Great Void, thus:—

"आद्य देवमाता शून्य वरदाता महाकु, शून्यटि कहि।" (१४ अध्याय)।

"परम-आत्माटि महाशून्य वोलि भाव।" (२२ अध्याय)।

"The primordial mother of the gods, the bestower of boons upon Çūnya, is herself known as the Çūnya." "Think of the Paramātman itself as the Mahā-Çūnya."

It is clear and evident from the Gītās of Mahādeva Dāsa and Balarāma Dāsa that the Buddhist Vaisṇavas of Utkala were divided between two camps of faith. According to one, Dharma, designated as Nirañjaña, was the first cause of the universe and his form was Çūnya or Void. Not unlike the followers of the Dharma-cult of the Rāḍha country who have associated and mixed up the following description of Viṣṇu with the *dhyāna* of Mahā-Çūnya—" शुक्लाम्बरधरं देवं शशिवर्णं चतुर्भुजं। प्रसन्नवदनं ध्यायेत् सर्ब्बविघ्नोपशान्तये ॥" "For the alleviation of all troubles and distresses one should call upon the four-handed god, clad in a white piece of cloth and having the colour of the moon and a graceful countenance"—they, too, incorporated the description contained in the above line with their mystic syllable "ओं शून्यब्रह्मणे नमः" "Om, salutation to the Çūnya Brahman." The other camp regarded and worshipped Dharma as a female divinity. Just as the image of Dharma is a highly sacred object in Nepal and is worshipped in every Chaitya there, so in the Chaityas of Mayūrabhañja, Dharma, was enshrined and worshipped in the female form. In the beginning of the Eighteenth Century the Tibetan pilgrim, Buddhagupta Tathāgatanātha, witnessed this worship in that place. In the vicinity of Haribhañja Chaitya, visited by this Tibetan pilgrim, we also discovered, in the course of our exploration, a similar stone-figure of Dharma.

NIRVĀNA.

We have found in the long extract made above from the Dharmagītā that the author used the words Nirvāṇa and Mahāçūnya as synonyms for Vaikuṇṭha.* Now, the term Nirvāṇa has been

* "स्वयं निर्व्वाण जे कल हृषिकेशो।
ते शून्य साहसे अन्तरिक्षे चाख दिशि।
से स्थान सबुझ शुद्ध बैकुण्ठभुवन॥"

explained by many scholars as the complete annihilation of being; and this is also the interpretation that obtains among the people. But it is not corroborated by Dharmagītā, according to which the term is neither negative nor privative but a positive one, denoting no annihilation of being but the essence of it. And this is just the view that Mr. Suzuki adopts in his Mahāyāna Buddhism. Thus he says.—

"The Mahāyāna Buddhism was the first religious teaching in India that contradicted the doctrine of Nirvāṇa as conceived by other Hindu thinkers who saw in it a complete annihilation of being; for they thought that existence is evil, and evil is misery, and the only way to escape misery is to destroy the root of existence, which is nothing less than the total cessation of human desires and activities in Nirvāṇic unconsciousness. The Yoga taught self-forgetfulness in deep meditation, the Sāṁkhya, the absolute separation of Puruṣa from Prakriti, which means undisturbed self-contemplation; the Vedānta, absorption in the Brahman, which is the total suppression of all particulars; and thus all of them considered emancipation from human desires and aspirations to be a heavenly bliss, that is Nirvāṇa."*

In his Nirākāra-Saṁhita Achyutānanda Dāsa declares Nirvāṇa to be the last stage of the religious life. He says—

"ब्रह्मानन्द येहु अदिव्य अव्यक्त दिव्यानन्द तहुं जाण ।
ताङ्क गुरुनाम सच्चिदानन्दटि स्वयं अनादि निर्गुण ।"

* D. T. Suzuki's Mahāyāna Buddhism, p. 340

"Know him who is Brahmānanda (who finds delight in the Brahman) to be the unrevealed Divyānanda. The name of his Guru is Satchidānanda, who is no less than the Anādi (without beginning or end) Nirvāṇa."

In fact, the several prominent Vaiṣṇava poets of Orissa, such as Balarāma Dāsa, Jagannātha Dāsa, Chaitānya Dāsa, Achyuta Dāsa, and Mahādeva Dāsa, in their respective works, use the terms 'Mahāçūnya' 'Çūnya Brahma,' 'Vaikuṇṭha' and 'Nirvāṇa' as conveying one and the same meaning.

ANUTTARA YOGA.

Abundant materials are on record to prove sufficiently that Anuttara Yoga or Haṭha Yoga obtained largely among the crypto Buddhists of Orissa. According to Lāmā Tāranātha, Tāntrism, which was only a popular but degraded form of Yoga, was transmitted from the time of Asaŋga and Dharma-kīrti. While endorsing the above view Dr. Kern[1] writes, "After Dharmakīrti's time the Anuttara Yoga became more and more general and influential." The religious works by Balarāma Dāsa and others furnish proofs in favour of this opinion. The Buddhists as well as the Çaivas regard Gorakṣanātha as the founder of the Haṭha-Yoga system. The Vaiṣṇava-Buddhistic work, entitled Amara-paṭala opens with a prologue containing a dialogue between Gorakṣanātha and Mallikānātha. The works by Achyutānanda and Balarāma, too, pay a sufficient homage to Guru Mīnanātha, Guru

Gorakṣanātha,* Mallikānātha, Vīrasiṁha, Lohīdāsa, Bāligā-dāsa and others.

BHAKTI AND BRAHMAVADA.

Dr. Kern justly observes—

"Mahāyānism lays a great stress on devotion, in this respect as in many others harmonising with the current of feeling in India which led to the growing importance of Bhakti. It is by the feeling of fervent devotion combined with the preaching of active compassion that the creed has enlisted the sympathy of numerous millions of people and has become a factor in the history of mankind, of much greater importance than orthodox Buddhism."†

The Oriya works of Balarāma Dāsa, Jagannātha Dāsa, Chaitanya Dāsa and Achyuta Dāsa are permeated with a spirit of devotion ; and there are many songs in these which display a high spiritual emotion. Besides, the Mahāyāna School indicates a conception of the Brahman which is based on the lines of the Vedānta Philosophy. "It would perhaps be more accurate to say that it is a pantheistic doctrine with a theistic tinge ; Buddha takes the place of the personified masculine Brahman of the Vedānta."‡

---

* Pag-sam-jon-zang (by Sumpo Khampo), a renowned Buddhist Scholar of Tibet) says "About this time (*i.e.* the 13th Century A D.) foolish Yogis who were followers of Buddhist Yogi Gorakṣanâtha became Civaite Sannyasis." Journal of the Asiatic Society of Bengal, for 1898, pt. 1. 5.

† Dr. Kern's Buddhism, p 124.

‡ Do. do. p 124 *note*.

The works of the above-mentioned authors abound with passages substantiating this construction. They show how Buddhism developed the idea of the Brahman, and how this Buddhistic ideal lastly evolved itself out in the creed of the later Vaiṣṇavas. The following extract from the Çūnya-Saṁhitā of Achyuta Dāsa will sufficiently illustrate this—

"परमे परम होइला गोपन आंश्रे कला अनादि कि ।
अलेखपुरे निरञ्जन पाटना दिव्यरूप तहि लेखि ॥
कालिन्दी कदम्बमूले देवगण सर्व्वाङ्गरु झाल झरे ।
रमाप्रेमाकुल चम्पकलतिता प्रेमलता प्रिय स्वरे ॥
शुभु अच्छि वाणी मधुर से ध्वनि पीयूष रस से रसे ।
महाशून्य यहिं रात्र दिवा नाहि कोटिसूर्य्य परकाशे ॥
देखिण अचेत हजिला सचेत जले जल गला मिशि ।
तेजरे तेज मिशिला त्रितपन वायुरे वायुटि मिशि ॥
पृथ्वी आप तेज वायव्य आकाश पञ्चात्मिक पञ्चजन ।
प्रत्यक्ष परम अक्षर अनाम महाशून्ये हेला लीन ॥
महाशून्य ज्योति अरूप अश्रुति रूप रेख यहिं नाहिं ।
हुताशन अग्नि महाशून्य होइ ज्योतिरानन्द वोलाइ ॥"

(२३ अध्याय)

"The essence is hidden in the primordial essence, the part is absorbed in the eternal whole. On the spotless Alekhapura is imprinted a divine form. On the bank of the Kālindī, under the Kadamba tree, the gods begin to shed lusters from their bodies. Hearing the sweet voice of

Champaka-lalitā and Prema-latā, Ramā is mad with love. The voice is as sweet as music, and as delicious as nector. In the Great Void where there is no day and no night, millions of suns begin to shine. I saw the animated world lost in the inanimate, water mixed with water, fire with fire, and air with air. The five senses made up of the five substances—earth, water, fire, air, and sky—became merged in the great eternal void without form and without name in my presence. The Great Void is effulgent, it has no sense of sight or hearing, there is not a single line or form in it. That brilliant Fire becomes the Great Void and is called Jyotirānanda (blissful light.)"

CRYPTO BUDDHISTS OF THE 16TH CENTURY.

The Mādhyamikas were absolute Anātmavādins (champions of the doctrine of non-egoism);* while the aforesaid devout poets were all of them Ātmavādins (followers of the doctrine of egoism) though they supported the doctrine of the void, for Paramātman, the great Ego or the Great Void, was, as the Brahman, the central idea about which all the effervescense of their devout poetic inspirations gathered. How then can these poets be regarded as Crypto-Buddhists?

It has been shewn in the beginning of this treatise that the ancient Buddhistic community came to be divided, in course of time, into various sects. Of these the Yogāchāra School believed in the existence of the soul or Ego,

* *Vide* Suzuki's Mahāyāna Buddhism.

but the others did not subscribe to this belief. We have also found that the Mādhyamikas looked with some disfavour and suspicion upon the Bodhisattvayānas or Çrāvakayānas, closely following the footsteps of the Sthavira Sect, because many of them were found to believe in the existence of the soul or Ego. It has further been noted almost at the outset that the sect of the Mantrayānas which sprang into existence about the fourth Century A.D. believed in the unification of the Jīvātman (individual soul) and the Paramātman (the universal soul). Nāgārjuna the expounder of the doctrine of the void and after him Diŋnāga, the great Buddhistic logician, had exercised great influences in Utkala. Even so late as the seventh Century when the Chinese pilgrim Hiuen Tsang (Yuan Chuang) came to visit India, he found here many remnants of their influences. Though in Oḍra he had found the Mahāyānists in all their glory and greatness, what he saw in Kaliŋga was but the Mahāyāna Sthavira Sect. The sect of the Hīnayānas sprang from the primitive Sthavira cult, and it is very likely that the Mahāyāna Sthavira Sect which came into existence in later times was simply the outcome of the union of these two into one. For long the voice of the Hīnayānas was the predominant one in Northern Bengal, and though in tho timo of the Pāla Dynasty many of them were forced to embrace the creed of the Mahāyānists, yet their original doctrines, ideas and beliefs were not altogether effaced; rather, they grew and were mixed up with their new acquisitions. We have already said that Nāgārjuna had accepted the theories and doctrines of the Gītā and the Upaniṣads. No wonder, therefore, that the Mantrayānas, who followed his creed, also accepted and tried to assimilate the Ātmavāda, doctrine of egoism, as expounded in the Gītā. Nepal was the chief abode of the Mahāyānists. After the principal Buddhist College of Nālanda was destroyed and razed to the ground on the conquest of the country by the Muhammadans, many of the Buddhist Çramaṇas of the place went to and took refuge in Nepal with their religious scriptures. The relics of these sacred writings are even now to be met with there. It was with the help of these and with the assistance rendered by one of Vajrāchāryas of the present Vajrayāna sect of Nepal, which is only a debased form of the Mantrayāna cult, derived in its turn from the Mahāyāna School, that Mr. Hodgson has been able to detect four different sects dividing amongst themselves the Buddhistic community of the place. The names of these four schools are Svābhāvikas, Aiçvarikas, Kārmikas and Yātnikas. Mr. Hodgson's remarks may be thus summed up—

The Svābhāvikas, apparently the oldest of the four schools, is again subdivided into two sects, *viz.*, Svābhāvikas simple and Prājñika Svābhāvikas. The former hold that nature or matter alone exists, engaged in an eternal evolution of entity and non-entity; while, according to the latter, matter in two modes, abstract or proper and concrete or contingent, is the sole substance. All the active and intelligent powers are unitised in the first mode, as inherent in matter, which is here deified and held to be unity, immutability, rest and bliss. The actual and visible nature, the scene of action, multiplicity, change and pain, is the result of the second mode. The first is called Nivṛtti and the second Pravṛtti. The powers of matter in their unity are indescribable; but in their concrete forms, *i.e.*, as nature, 'they are symbolised by the *yoni* and personified as a female divinity called Ādi-Prajñā and Ādi-Dharma.' Transmigrations are due to Pravṛtti, Nivṛtti producing eternal bliss. To attain this is the *summum bonum* (the highest good) of man.

In their interpretation of Nivṛtti, there is a division amongst the Aiçvarikas, some holding that 'Buddha represents intellectual essence and is the sole entity,' and others that 'Dharma or material essence exists with Buddha in Nivṛtti,' the two being inseparable there. When the essential principle of matter passes into the state of Pravṛtti, Buddha, the type of active power, first proceeds from it and then associates with it; and from that association results the actual visible world. The principle is feigned to be a female, first the matter and then the wife of Buddha.

The Kārmika School is so called from the word Karma, 'meaning moral action,' and the *yātnika* from the word *yatna*, signifying intellectual force, skilful efforts.' They are simply later developments of and supplements to the first two schools. Both the Svābhāvikas and the Aiçvarikas had in their own ways 'assigned that eternal necessary connection of virtue and felicity in which they alike believed.' The Kārmikas and the Yātnikas did not raise this question but confined themselves 'to the phenomena of human nature, its free-will, its sense of right and wrong and its mental power—to the wisdom of Svabhāva or Prajñā or Ādi-Buddha.' There were two questions here—Is that connection to be realized by man by 'the just conduct of his understanding?' or, is it to be realized by 'the proper cultivation of his moral sense?' In reply, the Yātnikas stood for the understanding and the Kārmikas for the moral sense, and thus they removed "the obloquy so justly attaching to the ancient Prājñika and even to the Aiçvarika School, because of the want of providence and of dominion in their first cause." Çākya gives the following descriptions of Karma and Yatna in Divyāvadāna, "The Union of Upāya and Prajñā is Karma, while Yatna is produced by Içvara (*i.e.*, Ādi-Buddha) from Prajñā or Nivṛtti, and all the difficulties that occur in the affairs of this world or of the next are rendered easy by Yatna." Impersonality and quiescence of the first cause with which the Svābhāvikas and the Aiçvarikas were charged were removed by these two schools by attributing free-will to man and moral attributes to God. The Kārmikas believe that fate is their own creation "पूर्व्वजन्मकृतं कर्म तद्दैवमिति कथ्यते."

Just as in Nepal the whole Buddhistic community is found at present to have been divided into four different sects, so in Utkala, after the destruction of Nālanda, the resident Buddhists were divided into several prominent sects, all springing up as results of the contact they successively came in with the different phases of Buddhism. Even so late as the 16th Century traces of their quondam influence and relics of their scriptures were discernible in Utkala. Achyutānanda Dāsa has thus referred to these schools in his Çūnya-Saṁhitā—

"नागान्तक वेदान्तक योगान्तक जेते ।
नाना प्रति विधिरे कह्हिले तोष चिते ॥
गोरखनाथङ्क विद्या वीरसिंह आज्ञा ।
मल्लिकानाथङ्क योग बाउलौ प्रतिज्ञा ॥
लोहिदास कपिलङ्क साक्षिमन्त्र जेते ।
कहिले जे येमन्त से होईछि गुपते ॥" (१० अध्याय)

" The Nāgāntāka (followers of Nāgārjuna), the Vedāntaka, (or Sautrāntika Schools) and the Yogāntaka (or Yogāchāra School)—all these have laid down, with all the sincerity of their faiths, various laws and bye-laws of conduct. The system of religious observances and practices inaugurated by Gorakṣanātha and the command of Vīra Siṁha, the Yoga system of Mallikānātha, the doctrine of the Bāuli or Bāula Sect, and the Sākṣimantras of Lohidāsa and Kapila—all these have been buried in secrecy."

Now, on the strength of these lines we can safely assert that Nāgāntaka or the Mādhyamika

Philosophy introduced by Nāgārjuna, the Yogāchāra or the system of rites and observances closely akin to those of Yoga as introduced and enjoined by Asaŋga and others, and the time-honoured school of Buddhism, called Sautāntrika, dealing with ancient Sutras or Buddhistic dogmas based upon the Upaniṣads—these three schools of thought; and the Haṭha-Yoga systems introduced and propagated by Gorakṣanātha* and Mallikānātha who flourished in later times, the doctrines of the Bāula sect, and the mantras introduced by Lohidāsa,† and Kapila—all these were all along alive and active, though driven underground by the force of many antagonistic circumstances. We take the Aiçvarika, Kārmika or Yātnika School of thought which obtains among the Buddhistic community of Nepal, to be but the latest phases of the Yogāntaka School of philosophy (which is in reality an attempt at a compromise between the ancient Yogāchāra

---

* Guru Goraksanātha was a disciple of Minanatha otherwise known as Matsyendra. The memory of the latter is worshipped by the Newar Buddhists as being the tutelary deity of Nepal. In the history of Tibetan Buddhism Goraksanātha occupies a very prominent place, being honoured and worshipped as one of the principal Buddhist sages. We learn from the pen of Lāma Tāranātha, historian of Buddhism, that the whole sect of the disciples and followers of Goraksanātha embraced the cult of Caivism in the thirteenth century A D. Even now he is held in great esteem and deified as Civa by the Yogi class. It has been hinted at in Cunya-Samhitâ that both he and Mallikânâtha were *Yoga-rurhas*, *i.e.* staunch adherents of the system of Yogāchāra.

† In the religious books of the Dharma cult of Rārha, Lohidāsa has been referred to as Lohichandra or Luhichandra. In Cunyapurâna we find an allusion to the worship of Dharma or Cunya by Rājā Hari-chandra, father of Lohichandra, and Madanā his mother. Mention is made in Cunya-Samhitā also of the *pravrajyā*, *matha* and Nirakāra-Dhyāna resorted to by Lohidāsa, and the reverse mode of Sādhana (devotion and prayer) after the principles of 'Nâgântaka' or Nâgârjuna.

and the Vedānta Philosophy), and the Svābhāvika or Prājñika Svābhāvika School, also to be met with there, survived as the Nāgāntaka School of Orissa—being a later development of the Mādhyamika School inaugurated by Nāgārjuna. It also becomes clear and evident even from Çūnya-saṁhitā that in the 16th Century A.D., Utkala was largely under the influence of the Mahāyāna School in its two branches of Yogāchāra and Mādhyamika. Besides, it has been clearly established from the Viṣṇugarbha of Chaitanya Dāsa and the Dharmagītā of Mahādeva Dāsa that the worship of the Pañcha-Dhyāni Buddha which even now obtains among the Newar Buddhists and the worship and narration of the traditional story of Dharma introduced by Rāmāi Paṇḍit in the time of the Pāla Kings, were in vogue in Utkala at the time. To escape the persecution and oppression which followed in the reign of Rājā Pratāparudra, upon the Buddhists of all sects and schools, a large majority of them embraced the Gauḍīya phase of Vaiṣṇavism of Lord Çrī Chaitanya. But it does not seem likely nor is it reasonable to expect, that all of them were earnest and sincere converts to the later Vaiṣṇavism of Gauḍa. On the contrary, we hope, it would not be too much to infer and assert that though many of them gave themselves out to be devout Vaiṣṇavas and staunch and loyal devotees of Mahāprabhu, yet they were, in their heart of hearts, but votaries of Buddha. And we can safely count Achyutānanda, Balarāma Dāsa, Jagannātha and Chaitanya Dāsa, referred to before, among this class of Vaiṣṇavas. Achyutānanda has himself thrown a flood of side light upon this in his Çūnya-saṁhita. It is related in his Nirākāra-Saṁhitā that implicitly obeying the direction of Çrī Chaitanya, Achuytānanda first became a convert to Vaiṣṇavism under Sanātana Gosvāmi and following the custom and practice of this sect, he put on all their outward marks. Referring to himself in his work he says that shortly after his conversion to Vaiṣṇavism, he could in no way bring his mind to take any the least interest in mundane matters. With the lapse of time this tendency became more and more marked, and his parents grew more and more dissatisfied and disgusted with him. Thus the only bonds that tried to tie him down to the concerns of the world, broke asunder of themselves, making him quite loose and free to follow the dictates of his own soul. In course of time the Nirguṇa made Himself manifest to him, illumining the innermost recesses of his heart and calming and pacifying the storm of passion and desire. At length, ten years and ten months after his conversion, at the foot of the western banian tree and in the village of Tripura on the bank of the river Patanā, he was graced by the presence of his Guru Brahma in his naked and untrimmed sublimity. His name was 'Mahānanda'. The mighty preceptor initiated him into the secrets and mysteries of religion and explained to him that the ultimate object of devotion, upon which alone the mind was to be concentrated, with reference to the attainment of which the whole life was to be regulated, and which was greater than the greatest of the preceptors, was 'Sachchidānanda' 'Anādi Nirvāṇa.'*—a stage where it is all eternal life, eternal bliss and consciousness. A short while after this Achyuta came to the forest of Daṇḍaka, on the eastern bank of the Prāchī and visited many Ṛṣis and Tapasvins (hermits, sages and ascetics). The misunderstandings and dissensions, which prevailed among these, have not been passed over in silence in Cūnya Saṁhita. About a week after this, at dead of night and in the heart of a dense forest, he was graced with the presence of Lord Buddha. Achyuta has thus alluded to him in his Çūnya Saṁhitā :—

"For five or seven days I walked into the dense forest in search of my Lord. One day at dead of night when I was deeply absorbed in studying the details of those who have met him and who have not, I was graced with His presence. He said 'Long and tedious has been the separation between myself and the five souls of my life. I would not rest till I met you.' Having heard this, I fell prostrate at His feet, cried aloud "Saved, O I am saved now !'. and informed Him of all the thoughts and ideas of my mind. Having heard me, the Lord burst into a fit of laughter and said 'Listen, Achyuta, to what I say. In the Kaliyuga, I have made myself manifest again as Buddha. It is desirable, however, for you in the Kaliyuga to hide your Buddhistic frames of mind away from view. You (five) are indeed

* Vide Nirâkâra Samhitâ.

my five souls, my five lives. Having undergone incarnation, I have found you back. All troubles and calamities will now be put an end to by means of the Nirākāra-mantra (devotion to formless Brahman or Çūnya). Having saved yourselves first by this, you will save others afterwards. I tell you, take refuge in Buddha,—in mother Ādi-çakti or the first primordial energy (*i.e.* Dharma) and in the Saŋgha* (congregation). By devoting yourself to the Nirākāra, you will be chastened and purified with an influx of piety, all pure and transparent. Having said all this, He initiated me into the religion of the Nirādhāra, (self-sustained) and instructed me to go back into the world and propagate this religion (as the means of salvation) in this Kaliyuga. The Lord said also "Know that Buddha is none else but Brahma Himself. And in this form do I dwell inside all bodies. Go, Ye Achyuta, Ananta, Jaçovanta, Balarāma and Jagannātha, go and publish what I say to you." Having been thus ordered, we five, instead of going to Manayāna entered the forest when Ṛṣis and Tapasvins, the Sannyāsins, the followers of Vīra Siṁha, Rohidāsa and Kapila, and the Bāula sect, all these bodies gathered together in an assembly, and there made known the wishes and directions of the Lord. I explained to them the Mantra, Yantra and Karanyāsa, appropriate to the Çūnya or Void. Upon this all the sages blessed themselves and blessed the name of the Lord. They then under-

---

* By many of the later ill-informed writers *Sangha* was change into *Sankha*.

stood that Çūnya Brahma, devoid of all forms, Himself resides as light, inside all bodies. The moving and the stationary, the insect and the fly, inside all these are the Çūnya Puruṣa, and the Çūnya Yantra. The Nirākāra (formless) Yantra which is the essence (emblem ?) of the Çūnya-puruṣa, who is a helpmate of the meek in spirit, has revealed all this out of great kindness."†

---

† "पाञ्च सात दिनरे प्रवेश हेउ याइ'।
गहने खट्ट प्रभु नियोगरे याई॥
निश्चि अर्द्धभागेन पड़इ तारतम।
कि पाइला न पाइला प्रभु नियोगेण॥
अवधान होन्ति मनु जनमाने पाइ।
एहि समयकु ये दर्श न करु' याइ॥
बोइलि मो प्राण पञ्च शाखा काहिं थिल।
नियोग न रुचे मोते तुम्भेत गइल॥
एहा शुणि थरथर तलि मु' पड़िलि।
निस्तरिलि निस्तरिलि बोलिण बोइलि॥
जनाइलि कासुरे सकल कथा मुहिं।
शुणिण उठिले प्रभु टह टह होइ॥
बोइले अच्युत तुम्भे शुण आम्भ बाणी।
कलियुगे बुद्धरूपे प्रकाशिलु पुणि॥
कलियुगे बौद्धरूपे निजरूप गोप्य।

*   *   *   *   *

तुम्भे मोर पञ्च आत्मा अट पञ्च प्राण।
अवतार श्रेणी येते तुम्भ पाइ' पुण॥
निराकार मन्त्रे सर्ब्ब दुर्गति हरिव।
आपने तरिण से ये परे तराइव॥
वुद्ध माता आदिशक्ति संघ अछन्ति कहि।
निराकार भजने निर्म्मल भक्ति पाइ॥

There can now be no shadow of a doubt about the fact that the five great souls, *viz.* Jagannātha, Balarāma, Achyuta, Ananta and Jaçovanta Dāsa, who have up till now generally passed for devout Vaiṣṇava poets, were in the sixteenth century the 'five lives' of the Buddhists *i.e.* mighty pillars of the great structure of the crypto Buddhistic community of Utkal. They acknowledged and sang the glory of the Trinity. We have already quoted, in connection with the

---

एमन्त कहि से देले मन्त्र निराधार ।
आज्ञा देले कलियुगे कर या प्रचार ॥
चिन्तिव कहिले प्रभु स्वयं ब्रह्म एहि ।
मुहिं एहि रूपे अच्छि सर्ब्ब घटे रहि ॥
याउ अच्युत अनन्त यशोवन्तदास ।
वलराम जगन्नाथ कर या प्रकाश ॥
आज्ञा पाइ आम्भे पाञ्च जन ये आइलु ।
मनयान न चलिला वने प्रवेशिलु ॥
ऋषि तपि सन्न्यासी नामक वीरसिंह ।
रोहीदास बाउली कपिल येते सङ्ग ॥
सभा मण्डाइण ये वसिले सर्ब्ब तपि ।
पचारिले प्रभुङ्क कि आज्ञा होइ अच्छि ॥
कहिलि मुं शून्य मन्त्र यन्त्र करन्यास ।
तपिमाने जय जय कले ये प्रकाश ॥
देखिले ये शून्य ब्रह्म स्वयं ज्योति होइ ।
घटे घटे बिजे एहि शून्यकाया देही ॥
स्थावर जङ्गम कीट पतङ्गादि येते ।
शून्यकाया शून्ययन्त्र बिजे घटे घटे ॥
शून्य कायाकु ये निराकार यन्त्र सार ।
भला दया कले दीन जनङ्क सोदर ॥ "

(शून्यसंहिता १० अध्याय)

history of the Bāthuri tribe the Çūnya or Dharma Gāyatrī that is to be found in the 'Siddhānta-ḍambara' of Balarāma Dāsa. There also the meditation upon or the mental recitation of, this trinity of Buddha, Dharma and Saŋgha are hinted at, as the means of salvation. The Manayāna that is alluded to in Çūnya Saṁhitā, seems to be but another form of the name, 'Mantrayāna.' Achyutyānanda said that in his time the influence of the Manayāna or Mantrayāna sect had considerably dwindled; and it was for this that the images of gods which were originally all of the mind, or to be realised from the mantras, had been reduced to images of wood, stone or earth, rendering it impossible to realise any longer their true natures and characteristics. And it was for this degeneration that Bhagavat propagated through the medium of these five men, the doctrine of the Çūnya Brahman putting on the guise of Buddha, for the salvation of the sinner and the sufferer of the Kali-yuga. Though they were sincere Buddhists, being votaries of Buddha, yet they found it necessary, nay unavoidable, to keep their Buddhistic frames of mind hidden under the guise of Vaiṣṇavism—for fear of the persecutions by the Brāhmaṇas and Kings. It is for this that we find the following line in Achyutānanda's Çūnya Saṁhītā—

"कलियुगे बौद्धरूपे निजरूप गोपर" ।

"It is desirable in the Kaliyuga that the followers of Buddha should be disguised."

INCARNATION OF BUDDHA.

Not only Achyuta Dāsa but almost all the ancient poets of Utkala when singing of the ten incarnations, have referred to Jagannātha or the Dāru-Brahma as being one and the same with the incarnation of Buddha, the saviour of men in the Kali-yuga.*

Vyāsa also expressed in his Bhāgavata Purāṇa (1.3.24)—

"ततः कलौ संप्रवृत्त संमोहाय सुरद्विषाम्।
बुद्धनाम्नाञ्जनसुत कीकटेषु भविष्यति।"

"Then on the advent of Kaliyuga, for the purpose of misleading the Asuras, the Lord will be born in Kīkaṭa as son to Añjana, and named Buddha."

But the devout poet Jagannāth Dāsa did not subscribe to this; he affirmed, on the contrary, in the fifth skandha of his Bhāgavata :—

"प्रबुद्ध बुद्ध अवतारे। ज्ञानविस्तारि ए संसारे॥
वेदर धर्म्म छड़ाइवे। निर्गुण धर्म्म प्रचारिबे॥
करणि न करिबे पुन। एनु ए मायार धेयान॥
पुन एमत समयरे। सिद्ध अन्न हेब घरे घरे॥
सकल वर्ण एक ठारे। बसि भुञ्जिब सुगतरे॥"

* Thus the poet Sâraladâsa says in his Mahabharata,

"नवमे वन्दइ श्रीबुद्ध अवतार।
बुद्धरूपे विजे कले श्रीनीलकन्दर॥"

"In the ninth I pay my humble respects to the incarnation of Buddha who in the form of Buddha dwelt in the Nîlâchala *i.e.* Puri."

" Coming down to the world as the all-wise Buddha, the Lord will diffuse knowledge, give up the religion inculcated in the Vedas and promulgate the doctrine of the Nirguṇa. None will then worship māyā again. And at this time, all the different castes will again sit together when partaking of boiled rice."

The purport of the lines is this. For the diffusion of real knowledge, for the setting aside of the vedic forms of worship and for the introduction and promulgation of the worship of the Nirguṇa Brahma—Buddha's incarnation will take place. Would any Paurāṇika Hindu save a pious and sincere follower of Buddha, acknowledge that it was Buddha who diffused real knowledge and introduced the worship of the Nirguṇa? Chaitanya Dāsa in his Nirguṇa-māhātmya while singing of the glories of the twelve Avatāras has found more or less fault with all the other eleven incarnations. It was only Buddha whom he found all pure and stainless. Thus he says of Buddha—

"बहुत बुद्ध अवतारे। हरि जन्मिले ए संसारे ॥६९
यज्ञ धर्म्म निन्दा कले। ब्रह्मज्ञान कि प्रशंसिले ॥७०
सकल धर्म्म दूर करि कर्म्मर फल अनुसरि ॥७१
अनेक कर्म्म धर्म्म फल। यज्ञ तप व्रत फल ॥७२
याग तर्पण आदि करि। ए सर्ब्ब एक तुल्य धरि ॥७३
धर्म्म तरु ये कलियुग। आउकि ब्रह्मज्ञान एक ॥७४
सकल धर्म्म आड करि। आउकि ब्रह्मज्ञान धरि ॥७५
से ब्रह्मज्ञान यत आड़े। भ्रमइ न छाड़न्ति दाड़े ॥७६
नेर्ब्बे आउके खुड़ि तरु। आर आउ थि जिर्ण मरु ॥७७

ए भावे तुंहि रचा करि। ब्रह्मज्ञानकु हृदे धरि ॥७८
सकल धर्म्म उपेचिली। ब्रह्मज्ञानकु साध्य कलै ॥७९
योगध्यानरे स्थिर मन। राखिल्लि ब्रह्मज्ञाने मन ॥८०"

"Incarnated as many Buddhas, Hari came down into the world. He found fault with the jajña-dharma, *i.e.* religion based upon sacrifices, offerings and oblations, and expressed himself highly in favour of (the attainment of) the knowledge of Brahman (as the basis and essence of religion). Holding works, religious practices, sacrifices, austerities, religious vows, *tarpanas* &c., equally useless with respect to the fruits they are expected to yield, he followed simply the sequence of actions accepting their results unaffected in the least.

"The Kali-yuga is like a tree of religion of which the knowledge of Brahma is the only root. Discarding all the other religions, he clung to the root, *viz.* knowledge of Brahman. Those who have not attained this knowledge, will wander from door to door in ignorance. So one (craving for salvation) will have to uproot all other decaying trees and all the other evil practices which have struck root in his mind. In this way only can he save himself, concentrating his mind all the while upon the knowledge of Brahman. Buddha discarded all the other forms of religion and only attempted, heart and soul, to attain the knowledge of Brahman, settling down his mind by practising *yoga* and *dhyāna* and concentrating it upon the knowledge of Brahman."

We can very thoroughly understand from the above extract in what light Jagannātha or Buddha was held by these devout poets.

SANGHA OR THE CONGREGATION.

From the Çūnya Saṁhitā we have gleaned the names of the places where these crypto Buddhists dwelt, as also the names of their leaders and their numbers as stated below :*—

Names of Places.	Names of Chiefs	Number of disciples.
Anantapur Câsana on the bank of the Prâchi ...	Dvija Krisnadâsa Mahâpâtra ...	1000
On the banks of the Madhurâ ...	Bhagavân of the Yadu Dynasty, and Gopa Daitâri ...	......
About Kuntinagara, Kâçipura, Kâlâgni, and Rukunâ Chaurâ ...	....	140
Kāçi Muktiçvara (a village near Bateçvara)	....	......
The village of Nembâla on the Chitrotpalâ ...	Achyutânanda	255
North to the (place of the) Pândavas ...	Ananta, Dvija Ganeça Pati, Kantha Ganak and Dvija Sâranga	200 (Dâsas) 300 of the Yadu dynasty.
On the bank of Brâhmani ...	....	300
Vâjanagara on the Vaitarani ...	Bandhu Mahânti ...	300
Varâha-mandala on the Vaitarani ...	Jagadânanda Agnihotri ...	300

Achyutānanda says that thus veiling themselves in innumerable ways three thousand†

---

* Çûnya Samhitâ, Chaps. XVII-XX.

† We find in Chapter XIX of Çûnya Samhitâ :—

"आउ भकत येते मोर अच्छन्ति बच्छिवा पद्मटीकारे ।
ठिके पाञ्च शत गुपत करिलु' हेतु कर तु मनरे ॥"

"From Padmatikâ you will know the names of the remaining votaries

votaries of Buddha were passing their days. Afraid of Kali, they were eagerly and anxiously waiting for the day when their Lord would again come down and reveal himself in all his glory. One and all of these Buddhists firmly believed that for the propagation of the religion based upon the knowledge of Brahman, Bhagavat Buddha would again be incarnated. This belief is expressed by Achyutānanda in the following lines :—

"कमलाङ्क अंशी जनमिबें आसि कलिरे हेब उदय ।
बारणबेले चिन्हाचिन्हि करिबें आपे प्रभु देवराय ॥
मथुरारे आसि आपे ब्रह्मराशि बउधरूप कलिरे ।
तिन सहस्र निज अंश ताहाङ्कर तेजिबें प्रभु कि परे ॥"

"In the Kali-yuga a part of Kamalāŋka will come down into, and be born in, the world. After incarnation, He and His devotees will recognise one another. In the Kali-yuga Brahman will first of all come to Madhurā, as Buddha, and will leave behind Him three thousand parts (*i.e.* faithful and devoted followers) of Himself."

---

of mine. For certain reasons known to myself, the names of just 500 devotees are kept concealed."

We are sorry, however, that the Padmatika work referred to above has not been found by us. It is very likely that further glimpses into the history of the crypto Buddhists of the 16th Century will be obtained when this work will be brought to light.

CHAPTER IV.

BUDDHISM IN THE SEVENTEENTH CENTURY.

Many facts have recently come to light which will go far to prove that though in the 17th Century Buddhism was generally considered to have fallen below the horizon, yet its setting beams were still lingering over and illumining many parts of the country. Lt. Col. Waddel the wellknown historian of Lāmāism has brought out an English translation of the accounts of the travels of Buddha Gupta Tathāgatanātha, written in the Tibetan tongue. It was early in the beginning of the 17th Century *i.e.* in 1608 that this great Buddhistic pilgrim came on a visit to India. We cannot do better than quote the following, two passages from the English translation of his account:—

"Thence (*i.e.* from Sambuddha) he went to Bengala *via* Jagannāth and Trilinga: thence to Pundravartagarasalini from which in twenty days he reached the shrines Kasramagaram and Devikotta in the upper part of Tripura where he remained in the monastery formerly built by the great Siddha Kronākara. He also visited Haribhanja, Phukrād and Palgar. In these countries the clergy and the books were numerous and the religion prosperous. While there, he heard a variety of esoteric teachings from the life (lips ?) of a great Pundit named Dharma of the Haribhanja Chaitya and believed to be a pupil of great Siddha, and also found a Pandita Upasika Hetagarbaghanna. He also visited . . . . chaitya and he saw the magic circles of Janakāya and Siddhānya Kaḍaka.

"On returning to India proper, Buddha Gupta visited Trilinga Vidyānagar, Karṇāṭaka and Bhamdoor. At the latter place he met the great Siddha Santagupta. Henceforth the pilgrim Buddhagupta is known as Buddhaguptanāth and he was especially empowered by the Jogin Dinakara and the great Guru Gambhīramati and he had taken instructions from the superior Uttara Suddhigarva and Gantapa, Belātikshana Bhirabandhu and Ghaghopa all of whom were followers of the aforesaid great Siddha Santagupta. He then went to Mahābodhi in the middle country and made a small house for meditation close to the north of Vajrāsana. Afterwards he visited the eight great shrines and Gridhrakuta Giriguphā and Prayāga. Forty-six years had now elapsed since his last meeting with Tirthanāth. Then he built an assembly house on Khagendra hill to which many Yogis resorted and he received royal patronage."

Thus we find that even in the Seventeenth Century there were to be seen a large number of the ministers of Buddhism, of both sexes, and possessing great supernatural powers,—at Haribhañja, Phukrāḍ and Pālgarh; and many Buddhistic scriptures of importance were also to be met with there. Let us now try to find out the exact situations of these places.

We learn from the aforesaid account that from Tipperah Buddhaguptanāth went to Haribhañja. When he came here in the 17th Century, the capital of Mayurabhañja was located at Hariharapur or Haripur. We are afraid there has been a confusion of names here, the name of the capital having been taken for the name of the whole country. Thus Haribhañja of the Tibetan traveller was no other than the old Mayūrabhañja. It had for a long time been the centre of Buddhistic influence. Here it was that Buddhaguptanāth visited the Haribhañja-chaitya; and it was here also that he learned many an esoteric truth from the lips of a great Dharma Paṇḍit and also from a Buddhistic Upāsikā named Hitagarbhaghanā.

Phukrāḍ or Phugrāḍ.—The Tibetan word *Phug* means the solitary dwelling place of the Lāmās for the purpose of meditation; and *Phugpa* means "a recess in a rock, a cave." Hence Phugrāḍ means a Rāḍha 'country' abounding in recesses or caves for the meditation of the Siddhas. As the entire province of Mayūrabhañja or for the matter of that, the hilly parts of it are known as Rāḍha to the people, it may not be unsafe to infer that Phukrāḍ, in the above account, refers to the hilly tracts of Mayūrabhañja interspersed with Siddha-guhās.

It is very likely that Pālgaḍa was but another name of the modern Pāllaharā, one of the eighteen Gaḍajāts or Feudatory States of Orissa. It is said that at one time the descendants of the Pāla Kings reigned here; and the ruins of Buddhism are still to be met with there in large numbers.

DISCOVERY OF A MODERN CHAITYA.

We should now try to find out the exact locality of the Haribhañja Chaitya, where Hitagarbha-Ghanā, the Buddhist Upāsikā, presided, where a vast number of Buddhist Çramaṇas lived and moved and many a religious book was read and taught, and where from far-off countries, students and observers flocked in large numbers to be initiated into the mysteries of the religion.

Both from the small Chaitya that has recently been discovered near Bodhipukhur in the village of Baḍasāi, and the materials that can be gathered from the place, it appears to be very likely that the ancient Haribhañja Chaitya must have been situated somewhere near it. One will invariably see in Nepal that wherever there was a big chaitya, there was also a large number of smaller ones about it and built in imitation of it. In Nepal the images of Ādi Buddha, Pañcha Dhyāni Buddha and Triratna (*i.e.* Buddha, Dharma and Saŋgha) are to be found enshrined in every Chaitya and by the side of each Chaitya are to be met with the statues of Hārīti and Çītalā. The small Chaitya discovered near Baḍasāi is known to the Hindus as Chandrasenā. It is considered to have been either the prototype or the foundation of a larger one. The following lines well express the general import of the chaityas :—

" The chaitya may be regarded as the foundation on which the ecclesiastical architecture of the Buddhists is based, and as supplying the model from which nearly all their principal temples whether they be dedicatory, memorial or funeral, have been constructed."

Thus writes Dr. Oldfield about the Buddhistic chaityas of Nepal—

"In almost all chaityas of whatever size, small as well as large, round the base of the hemisphere there are four niches or shrines—one opposite to each of the four cardinal points—in which are placed seated figures of four out of the five Divine Buddhas—Akṣobhya is enshrined in the eastern niche, Ratnasambhava in the southern, Amitābha in the western and Amoghasiddha in the northern. There is always a shrine to Vairochana."

In this model chaitya are to be found four figures in the four niches. They represent Akṣobhya and three other Dhyāni Buddhas with their Vāhanas and Bodhisattvas. By the side of this chaitya is an image of Dharma. Similar figures are also to be met with by the side of the majority of the chaityas in Nepal. In the following passages the reader will find an accurate description of this figure of Dharma :—

"Dharma's figure is always that of a female with prominent bosoms, two of her hands are brought together in front of her chest with the points of the fore fingers and thumbs in contact as in the Dharmachakramudrā of Vairochana; in a third hand she holds either a lotus flower or else a book containing the scriptures or law of Buddha; and in her fourth hand she has a Mālā or rosary of beads."

Chandrasenâ or a modern chaitya *from Badsâi*

"In a shrine at the Chillandeo temple, Kirtipur, the figure of Dharma, on the left of Buddha, has four hands of which two are empty, in the third is a book and in the fourth a rosary."*

This description of Dharma is exactly applicable in the case of the figure found at Baḍasai. Another figure of a similar description—but with two hands,—was also found in the Mahā Bodhi at Gayā, bearing inscriptions of the 12th Century A. D. In his Virāṭa Gītā, Balarāma Dāsa is found to have said "धर्मवर्ण हला शक्ति" *i.e.* 'Çakti or the creative power took the form of Dharma.' In Nepal she is also known as Guhyeçvari. At Baḍasāi the figure of Çītalā is to be seen close by the image of Dharma. This practice of enshrining the figure of Çītalā in close proximity of that of Dharma is also followed in Nepal. "The goddess Çītalā was universally believed to afford necessary protection to all who sought her aid. The Buddhists accordingly recognised her divinity and besought her protection; they enrolled her among the list of their subordinate deities and erected a temple to her honour beneath the very shadow of the temple of Ādi Buddha at Çambhunāth."

The existence of the model chaitya and the figures of Dharma and Çītalā afford us strong grounds for believing that at one time there was also a larger chaitya in the vicinity. These images had formerly been located in the close proximity of a tank, known as Bodhipukur, pro-

* Dr. Oldfield's Nipâl, Vol. II.

bably from the Buddhistic chaitya, and have only been recently brought into the village. Extensive corn-fields only are, however, to be seen now, rolling far and away from the embankments of the tank on all sides—no relics of the supposed ancient chaitya, no, not even a faint shadow of them, will now satisfy the longing gaze of the antiquary.

When the Tibetan pilgrim visited the country, the Bhañja Rājās had their capital at Haripur. From here Bodhipukur was only five miles off. Excepting the small chaitya and the image of Dharma that we came upon in the course of our exploration and antiquarian researches, no Buddhistic relics of any kind, of a modern chaitya were to be found in the locality. So it will not be very wide of the mark to infer, we presume, that the Haribhañja chaitya referred to by the Tibetan pilgrim, existed somewhere near Baḍasāi,—and here it was that he met with a Dharma Paṇḍita and received many esoteric instructions. In the course of our researches in the village we came across also some Oriya Mss. such as Siddhānta-ḍambara, Anākāra Saṁhitā, Amarapaṭala, and songs of Govinda Chandra, the great mendicant King of Bengal.

Thus these facts cannot but convince the most casual thinker that this place was once the centre of Buddhistic thought and activity.

Dr. Oldfield thus explains the views of the Buddhist Newars :—

"The Materialists (*i. e.* the follower of the ancient Mahāyāna system) assign the first place

Dharma *from Badsâi*

Citalâ *from Badsâi.*

in their Trinity to *Dharma*, as the spirit representing matter, from which everything in heaven or earth originally sprung.

"They deify Dharma as a goddess, under the names of Ādi-Dharma, Prajñā Devī, Dharma Devī, Ārya-Tārā; using any or all of these epithets as synonyms to signify the supreme, self-existent powers of *Nature*, whom they worship as the universal *Mother*, not only of all mankind, but of all the heavenly deities. All Buddhists are her children, and, therefore, all are brothers.

"The Materialists make Buddha subordinate to Dharma, and give him the second place in their trinity. They look on him as derived from Dharma, springing from her as a son from a parent, and then reacting upon her in some mysterious way, the result of which was the production of the Buddhas and of all other animated beings.

"Saŋgha, the Materialists regard as the type of all the forms of visible nature, which are produced by the creative power inherent to matter and which spontaneously result from the union and association of Dharma with Buddha."*

In the course of our sojourn at Baḍasāi† we came to learn that once there lived a caste known as 'Yogis' there. They had in their possession several Mss. treating of the Dharma cult. Their professional duty was to sing songs relating to Rājā Govinda Chandra and the praises of

* Dr. Oldfield's Nipal, Vol. II. p. 96-97.
† Vide Report on Badasâi.

Dharma. From Baḍasāi they migrated to the Nilgiri where they are even now to be found. We happened to find here in the house of a poor rustic a Ms. entitled "The Songs of Rāja Govinda Chandra" by Kālabhārati. Formerly it was the the property of an old Yogi resident of the place. We do strongly believe that if a thorough and sifting search be instituted for the purpose at Baḍasāi and the surrounding places, similar important manuscripts can be recovered from oblivion and impending destruction.

We have said above that in the course of our exploration in Baḍasāi we have found the figures of Dharma and Çītalā only. Now it may reasonably be asked—How is it that the images of Buddha and Saŋgha are not included in the group, if the place was, as asserted, a centre of Buddhistic influence? On this point, some are of opinion that these were removed or destroyed by the Mahomedans or the Marāṭhās. What, however, appears to us to be a more reasonable explanation is that in course of time a greater importance came to be attached to Dharma, and Buddha and Sangha happened to be relegated to less important places. When Dharma came to be worshipped in form, she was considered to be superior to Buddha and Saŋgha by a sect of the Buddhists. Thus in Svayambhū-Pūrāṇa she is addressed as follows—

"शून्यतां शून्यतां माता बुद्धमाता प्रकीर्त्तिता" ॥ (३ अः)

"The mother, the void of the great void is spoken of as the Buddhamātā."

In the Uriya Ms. of Çūnya Saṁhitā by Achyutānanda Dāsa it is said—

"वुद्ध माता आदिशक्ति सङ्घ च्छन्ति कहि ।" (१० अः)

" Thus I say, take refuge in Buddha, in Mātā Ādiçakti *i.e.* the primodial energy (Dharma) and in the Saŋgha."

Why Dharma is still worshipped and why Buddha and Saŋgha have been entirely cast in the shade, are sufficiently explained in these passages. Brāhmaṇas are not allowed to officiate in the worship of the above Dharma, Çitalā or Chaitya ; but worship is offered to these deities by the lower class of Dehuries. Formerly, only the Bāthuries were in enjoyment of this privilege and even now they are sometimes seen to officiate as priests at the pujās of these deities. The day of the full moon in Vaiçākha is a sacred day of the Buddhists. Throughout the whole Buddhistic world, it is observed in connection with the nativity, the spiritual enlightenment and the Mahāparinirvāṇa of Buddha. And on this Vaiçākhi-Pūrṇimā day worship is also offered to the abovementioned Buddhistic Chaitya, Chandra-Senā,* and a great festival is held. This practice has obtained for a long time past and is known in the locality as Uḍāparva. Some twenty to twenty-five thousand low class people muster there on the occasion, the Bāthuris, of course, forming the majority. Dressed as *Bhakats*, they

* That Chandra-sena is associated with Buddhism is unmistakably borne out by the Uriya poet Manohara Dâsa in his Amarkosa Gitâ. See p. ccxxxvi.

celebrate the ceremony of the Chaitya-Pūjā, suffer themselves to be pierced without a murmur with a hook, and merrily and lustily swing on the Chaḍaka.

A very great enthusiasm prevails on the occasion. Sometimes even so large a number as two hundred *Bhakats* vie with one another to have their bodies pierced with hooks—impelled by a strong and irresistible desire to have their vows to the effect literally fulfilled ; a piece of cloth is then tied round their bodies over the pierced parts, and lustily do they enjoy swings on the Chaḍaka post planted for the purpose. Even the public in general regard this festival held once annually, as a highly holy and dignified one. Even the Brāhmaṇas are second to no other castes in their regard and enthusiasm for this festival. Including, as it did, the worship of the images of the five divine Buddhas and the Bodhisattvas, it was an object of great sanctity and veneration to the Buddhists. In Nepal too, a similar worship is offered in the places in which similar figures have been enshrined.

At Baḍasāi the Chaitya is worshipped only once a year *viz.*, on the Vaiçākhī-Pūrṇimā day when the Uḍāparva is celebrated ; but the case of Çītalā is quite different. For long she has been frequently receiving the worship of the Hindus and the Buddhists alike. The figure of Çītalā now passes there for that of Kālikā, and for this reason even the Brāhmaṇas feel no scruples in worshipping her. But generally the worship of this deity is entrusted to the low class Dehuris, who have been in return for this service long enjoying the benefits derived from the property endowed and set apart for the performance of the worship.

Beside this chaitya and the images of Dharma and Çītalā, there are also to be found near Rāṇi-bandh only 3 miles off from Baḍasāi, beautiful figures of Khaṣarpaṇa Lokeçvara (Avalokiteçvara) and Ārya Tārā, and also an image of Jāŋgulī Tārā, near Haripur. These are the only remnants, that have been recovered, of Buddhism, and in a place where only two centuries and a half before there flourished many a Buddhistic upāsaka and upāsikā, where there flocked Buddhist priests and laymen even from Tibet and other distant places to have a view of the famous chaitya which once stood towering there, and where many a student came to obtain esoteric instructions, undeterred by the difficulties and obstacles that would encounter him on his way.

We have remarked, while dealing with Dharma Gītā, that its author, Mahādeva Dāsa, flourished in the 17th Century. As one of the results of a critical study of his work, one has to come to the irresistible conclusion that like Rāmāi Paṇḍit of Bengal, he also set his mind upon the extollation and promulgation of the glories and greatnesses, powers and potencies of Dharma as the sole object of his life. Though some minor differences may be observed in the histories of religious development in Rāḍha and Utkal due to differences in the natural constitutions of the two countries, the changes wrought upon them by time and the differences in the mental constitution of the people of the two provinces, extending over centuries, yet there can but be little doubt that originally these histories are but one and the same, just as much as the two branches of the same tree. And it seems to us that the Tibetan pilgrim referred to some such Paṇḍit as this Mahādeva Dāsa the author of Dharma Gītā. Further, it also seems very likely to us that the esoteric works, referred to by the Tibetan pilgrim are nothing but the religious books composed by Balarāma, Jagannātha, Achyutānanda, Ananta, Yaçovanta, Chaitanya, Mahādeva and others of their stamp.

We find sufficient traces of the great sway which the doctrine of Çūnya, discussed above at some length, once exercised upon the minds of men in the religious literature of the poets and gentlemen who hallowed and sanctified Utkala in this century or the century after. A study of such works as the Mahīmaṇḍala Gītā of Arakṣita Dāsa, the Çūnyarāsa of Nāraṇa Dāsa, the Brahmajñāna-Gītā of Paraçurāma Dāsa and the Nāma-Brahma Gītā of Dīnakṛṣṇa Dāsa will clearly convince any one of the truth of our assertion.

CHAPTER V.

THE REVIVAL OF BUDDHISM.

We have learnt from the various religious books of Utkala of the 16th, the 17th and even of the 18th century, that many crypto Buddhists were then residing in various parts of the country. In the hills and the forests of the Gaḍa-jats, they cherished the loving memory of their religion and made no secret of it amongst themselves, though, in society, they passed for devout Vaiṣṇavas. The Buddhist pilgrims of Tibbet and other far-off places who came on visits to India did, however, see through their veils and acknowledged them to be their co-religionists.

On this point, we have in the last Census Report, "In the 17th century Buddha-Guptanātha wandered in various parts of India and found Buddhism flourishing in many places. Then it is lost altogether. For two or three centuries Buddhism was absolutely unknown in India."*

We cannot, however, fully subscribe to the above statement. There is ample evidence to show that even after the 18th century Buddhism

* Census Report of Bengal, 1901, Pt. I., p. 203.

was not altogether a lost creed—the much-honoured memory of Buddha was not altogether a forgotten thing in India. We find in the Amarakoṣa of Manohara Dāsa written only hundred years back, the following line :—

"अर्ज्जुन बुद्ध हैले जीव परम हैले कृष्ण।"

"Arjuna *i.e.* Buddha is Jīva (the individual soul) and Kṛṣṇa is *parama* (*i.e.* the universal soul)."

While dealing with the Buddhist relics at Baḍasāi, we have noticed that there is a model Chaitya there, which is generally known by the name of 'Chandrasenā.' Of this Chandrasenā the same author says—

"चन्द्रसेना नामे एक दुयारि। घाट साधु अछि पथ आवरि॥
ताहा सङ्गे येवे परचे होइ। बुद्ध पाइले भितरक याइ॥"

"A door-keeper named Chandrasenā, who is also a tol-collector, is keeping watch upon the door. Any one, desirous of entering it, must make himself known to him. And if he be convinced that the visitor is a Buddhist, then and then only will he allow him admission."

Hence do we clearly see, that only so far as a century back the holy name of Buddha was on the lips of many crypto Buddhists who outwardly professed the Vaiṣṇava creed ; nay, they even recognised Buddha as Jīvātman or the individual soul.

From a careful study of the Buddhistic scriptures, whether of ancient or of much later times, we do learn that the Buddhists never passed themselves for such, nor did they ever designate their faith as Buddhism. In every page of the history of their religion, they are found to have called it simply Dharma or at most 'Saddharma' or 'Sadharma', and to have styled themselves as 'Dharmin' or 'Saddharmin'. Following suit, the Utkala community of the veiled Buddhists has given the name 'Mahimā-dharma' to its creed and styles itself as 'Mahimā-dharmin.' Under the benign spirit of religious toleration and the noble and fostering spirit of freedom of thought inaugurated and scrupulously adhered to by the British Government, this community has begun, for over 40 years, to rouse itself up, to throw off its masks and to re-assert itself duly. We shall attempt to give below a brief history of its struggle for renascence.

For long these Utkala Buddhists had been cherishing the happy belief, handed down from generation to generation, that Buddha would again grace the world in flesh and blood for the diffusion of knowledge and the propagation of true religion. For over four hundred years such devout souls as Achyutānanda, Yaçovanta, and others had been singing of this. And we have it on the authority of the subsequent writers that their prediction has been literally fulfilled.

We have come to learn from 'Alekha-līlā,'* a

---

* "वन्दइ अलेख ब्रह्म महाशून्ये स्थिति । परब्रह्मस्वामी यार चरणे अच्छन्ति ।"
(अलेखलीला)

"I make my obeisance to Alekha Brahman who dwells in the great void and at whose feet lies prostrate the Great Lord Para-Brahman."

religious book and also from the lips of many Mahāntas of this sect that about 50 years ago Bhagavat Buddha came down into the world. The subject of his worship was the Alekha-Brahma or the Great Void, and his object, the deliverance of the world. At first Bhagavat Buddha blessed the village of Golāsiŋgā in the State of Baud. Çrī Jagannātha also left Nīlāchala and came down to join him there. When Jagannātha was granted the interview he sought for, he asked of Buddha, "Would you please enlighten me on the points which have filled my heart with misgivings? Under whose direction and why have you come down as Guru?" And he replied "Then hear me, O Jagannātha (Lord of the world)—Under orders of Alekha, the Formless, I have come here. He, and none else, is the Great Void—the Formless One without a begining—the Highest of Gurus. The Kali has manifested itself everywhere. It is to destroy sin of the Kali-yuga that I have undergone incarnation.* Per-

---

* "येते वेळे बुद्धस्वामी मर्त्त्य विजे कले ।
काहाकु ये दीचा देइ मर्त्त्य विचरिले ॥
गुरुस्वामी ये मनरे जाणिले अन्तर्यामी ॥ ५
एकाम्बरो बुद्धस्वामी शून्यमार्गे गले ।
वउद ये गोलासिङ्गा ग्रामरे मिळिले ॥
बुद्धरूप ये, नवतन वेश कले गोफारे ॥ ६
नीलाचल तेजिण ये जगन्नाथ गले ।
गोलासिङ्गा भूमिर पाइ ये मठ कले ॥
रहिथिले ये, बुद्धस्वामी याइण भेटिले ये ॥ ७
जगन्नाथ कहुच्छन्ति शुणिमा गोसाइ ।

mit me, please, to initiate you into the doctrines of the true religion ; then for the good of humanity, go to Kapilāsa and remain stock-still in a trance" Upon this, he delegated all his powers to lord Jagannātha who, then, went away, as directed, to Kapilāsa in the Dhenkānal State. Here he came to be known by the name of Govinda. And here, for the good of humanity, he remained deeply absorbed in a trance for a period of full twelve years. His staple food, then, was simply a very small quantity of milk and fresh water. At the expiration of the trance, he descended from Kapilāsa, and for the propagation of the "Mahimā Dharma," blessed Bhīma Bhoi with 'the eye of knowledge' *i.e.* insight and self-consciousness. Then he disappeared, none knew whither, after having initiated into the true religion, many pious souls in Kapilāsa, Khaṇḍagiri, Maṇināga, and many other places.*

It is in many of the ancient religious books of Utkala that Jagannātha himself has been

---

तुम्भे केंहु गुरु मोते जनात न जाइ ॥
फेड़ि कह ये, ग्रथि मन फिटिब सन्देह ये ॥ ८
बुद्धस्वामी कहुच्छन्ति शुण जगन्नाथ ।
अलेख आज्ञारे आसि होइ उपगत ॥
महाशून्य ये, अरुप अनादि गुरुस्वामी से ॥ ९
कलिपाप भाष ये नाश हब सुमति ।
आम्भ तहुं अनेक प्रकारे कला उपति ॥
पापनाश ये, कलियुग समयर ह्रास ये ॥" १० इत्यादि

(अलेखलीला)

* According to some Buddha Svāmin again started the religious cycle in A.D. 1864.

described as the incarnation of Buddha. In view of this, the above quotation may well lead one to question, how is it that Jagannātha, who was himself Buddha, was initiated by Buddha? The answer is not far to seek, if we will only take the trouble for it. Holders of this faith do never say that there was only one Buddha. Like the Mahāyānists of yore they also admit of a multiplicity of the incarnations of Buddha. And in support of their view they quote the following lines, quoted by us previously, from the Nirguṇa-māhātmya of Chaitanya Dāsa—"वहुत बुद्ध अवतारे। हरि जन्मिले ए संसारे।" "Many were the incarnations of Hari as Buddha."

We find a detailed narration of this in the Buddhist Jātakas. We have shewn before, in connection with our treatment of the Pañcha-dhyāni Buddhas, that out of the lustre of the self-existent first Buddha came the Dhyāni Buddha; and out of the latter's came Bodhisattva. Dhyāni Buddha is engaged in a trance which is free from, and above, all illusions and doubts and it is Bodhisattva who fulfils and brings to realization all his wishes and desires for the good of humanity. So we may accept the Buddhasvāmin of Alekha-līlā as Dhyāni Buddha, and Jagannātha as Bodhisattva or Padmapāṇi.

And just as Çākya Buddha entrusted Ānanda with the task of propagating his 'Saddharma,' so Bodhisattva in the form of Govinda (Jagannātha) left the duty of propagating his Mahimā-dharma to his favourite disciple, Bhīma Bhoi.

Some of the adherents of this creed even hold that after Jagannātha had left Nīlāchala, he gave up his individual existence, and becoming one and the same with Buddhasvāmin in body and soul, went on with the task of more and more widening the circle of this religious movement. We find a detailed account in one of the scriptures of this sect, entitled Yaçomatī-mālikā, as to when, why and how this movement was set on foot and carried on by Buddha ; and we give just a glimpse of it to our readers by quoting at random from tho same* :—

(Garuḍa is addressing Jagannātha—)

"When wilt Thou that art the four-handed (Viṣṇu) incarnate Thyself in the form of Buddha of whom you have just spoken?

"Hearing these words of Garuḍa the Lord replied, 'Hear me, O Lord of birds, I shall explain this to you in detail. But, bear in mind, what I am going to tell you is *a very great secret*, and you must not open your lips to any body about it.' 4-6.

* * * * *

"Hear my child, I shall tell you all. I am anxiously waiting for the time when Kali-yuga will come to its close. In the forty-first year (of the reign) of Mukunda Deva, I shall give up

---

* "बुद्ध अवतार रूप वहिव ये याहा ।
केते वेले सेहिरूप हइब चौबाहा ॥ ४

this life as Buddha and disappear altogether. And when I shall renounce this body, all the gods will follow suit, for Hari, Hara, Brahmā and myself are but one; and my soul will live in that of the Alekha. 133-136. Then assuming a form with the help of māyā, I shall pass for an *avadhūta* and be worshipping the lord Alekha. Then Kali will arrive there, complete in its four parts, and Brahman of great lustre, though nothing but the void, will assume a form and be born in the world. And this new god, the realiser of the wishes and desires of men, will visit Khaṇḍagiri, Maṇināga and Kapilāsa. And satisfying his hunger and thirst with fruits, leaves of trees, milk and water, will be playing his various illusive tricks, the wide world over. But none, man or god, will be able to know when he will be

---

गरुड़ वचन शुणि प्रभु वलि मोर ।
शुण ताहा बुझाइ कहिबा पाचवर ॥ ५
अतिहि गुपत कथा कहि देवा तोते ।
कांहि न कहिबु एहा बुझि थाइ चिते ॥ ६" * * * *
"शुणरे नन्दन तोते देउअछि कहि ।
कलियुग शेष कतु थिबु वाट चाहि ॥ १३३
मुकुन्ददेवङ्क एकचालिशि अङ्करे ।
बुद्धरूपकु तेजि थिबु गुपतरे ॥ १३४
आम्भे येते बेलि पिण्ड त्यजिबुरे सुत ।
सकल देवता याक हेबे सेइ मत ॥ १३५
हरिहर ब्रह्मा एक अटइति मुं हि ।
निज आत्मा थिब मोर अलेखर तंहि ॥ १३६

born. 137-141. With the intention in his mind of playing a part with men upon the stage of the world, the Çūnyapuruṣa will undergo this incarnation—because the world will then be a hot-bed of vice and sin. Under my orders, many of his devotees have long been undergoing the pains of birth. In the incarnation as Buddha, he will play the rôle of Guru, preceptor, and will impart knowledge to and enlighten the minds of his disciples who will be known by the kumbhipaṭa (bark of a Kumbhi tree) they will put on. . . . . . 142-144. But veiled as he will then be, few but Bhīma Bhoi, his quondam follower, will be able to recognise him. He will first sing

---

माया काया धरि अबधूत बुलाइबु
अलेख प्रभुङ्क आम्भे सेबा करि थिबु ॥ १३७
चतुर पाद कलि आसि पुठिबाका महो।
महातेज ब्रह्म उदे हेवे शून्यदेही ॥ १३८
नवकल्पटारु प्रभु उदे हे थिवे।
खण्डगिरि मणिनाग कपिलास ठाबे ॥ १३९
फल पत्र क्षीर जल करिण आहार।
खेल खेलुथिबे प्रभु ब्रह्माण्डे याकार ॥ १४०
नर मनुष्य ये आदि देबलोक याए।
जानि न पारिवे केहि प्रभुङ्क उदये ॥ १४१
से शून्यपुरुष माने बिचार ये कले।
नर सङ्ग मध्ये खेला करिबु वहले ॥ १४२
महाघोर पातक हेब अबनीर।
भक्त मात छइछन्ति आज्ञा रे आम्भर ॥ १४३
बुद्धरूप भाव गुरुरूपे ज्ञान देबे।
कुम्भिपट देइ नाना प्रकाश करिबे ॥ १४४

the praises of the Lord and will attain the position and honour of becoming one and the same with Çūnya of the Alekha-maṇḍala. And thereafter, under the precepts of the Guru, pious men will sing the praises of the name of Mahimā —to their hearts' content." 145-147.

From the above quotation it is clear and evident that Jagannātha generally passed for Buddha till the 41st aŋka (year) of the reign of Mukunda Deva of Utkala. And we have learnt from the pen of the Tibetan Lāmā Tāranātha, a historian of Buddhism, that this Mukunda Deva was in reality a staunch and faithful worshipper of Buddha and was generally known by the name of "Dharma-rāja." It was during his time that the notorious Kālāpāhāḍa carried on his formidable crusade against Hinduism and Buddhism; and it was with the close of his long reign that the Buddhists began to pass their lives in concealment and seclusion. Behind the temple which now generally passes as the Temple of Sūrya Nārāyaṇa, and situated within the very precincts of the famous temple of Jagannātha, is a gigantic statue in stone of Buddha sitting in the Bhūmisparça-mudrā. Strange to say,

अतिहि ये चीणरूप न चिनिबे केहि ।
पूर्व्वर भकत ये चिनिव भीम भोई ॥ १४५
ताङ्क मुखे प्रभुङ्कर भजन हइव ।
अलेख मण्डल शून्यपद ये रहिब ॥ १४६
भक्त जने गाइ ताहा परम सन्तोषे ।
महिमा नाम गायन गुरु उपदेशे ॥ १४७ (यशोमतीमालिका)

a massive wall has been built up just in front of this statue, completely obstructing the view of it from outside. This statue, which could otherwise have spoken volumes of past history, has all along remained a sealed book to the majority of observers and visitors. We have, however, come to know, as the result of a very sifting investigation, that this temple dedicated to Buddha is much older than the chief temple of Jagannātha itself. It is not at all improbable that upon the close of the career of Rājā Mukunda Deva, the obstructing wall was built up to hide the statue from the public eye ; and it may also be the case that the tradition of the image of Jagannātha as Buddha being hidden from view dates its origin from this time.

MAHIMADHARMA OR NEW BUDDHISM.

The Brahmanic theory that when the pan of virtue is quickly kicked up, Bhagavat undergoes incarnation and comes down into the world to lighten the heavy burden of sin and vice, is also shared by the Mahāyāna Buddhists. So the belief in the birth and life of a Buddha is in no respect absurd or incongruous. The followers of the Mahimā-dharma creed do indeed consider themselves blessed when they point to Khaṇḍagiri, Maṇināga and Kapilāsa as being the places where this new Buddha displayed himself in all his glory and splendour.

In answer to any query as to the date of the commencement of this new religious movement under the name of Mahimā-dharma or 'New

Buddhism, the followers of the creed recite the following few lines from Yaçomatī-mālikā :—

"दिव्यसिंहदेवङ्क एकइश अङ्करे ।
अरिष्ट हइब जात ए कलियुगरे ॥ १६७
ऊनचिश अङ्कु ये शुण आरे वीर ।
अतिहि प्रबल युद्ध हइब निकर ॥ १६८
एकचाळिश अङ्करे हेब समापत ।
चौबन से पुन एक धर्म्म सत्य ॥ १६९
नीच कुळे भक्त कुळ हुयन्ति से जात ।
अलेख नामकु शुणि हइबे आश्रित ॥" १७०

"In the twenty-first aŋka (year) of the reign of Divya-Siṁha Deva, will a very sad event occur in the Kali-yuga, and in the twenty-ninth year a very terrible war will break out, as sure as anything, and will end only in the forty-first year—re-establishing the only true religion The devotee of this new creed, though of mean extraction, will, we hear, be in the special good graces of Alekha."

Thus we learn that the revival of Buddhism in the name of Mahimā-dharma took place in the twenty-first year of the reign of Divya-Siṁha, late King of Puri, *i.e.* in 1875. It was in this year that the devout Bhīma Bhoi,whose words were inspired, most solemnly declared to the world the truth and greatness of the Mahimā-dharma. And we have heard from the lips of the preceptors of this sect that it was about this time also that a large number of books, evidently written to establish the truth and high character of the religion, was discovered underground inside a large closed copper vessel. Chief amongst these are the works of Jagannātha. Balarāma, Achyutānanda, Yaçovanta and Chaitanya Dāsa.

THE SCRIPTURES OF MAHIMĀ DHARMA.

The reader will surely be interested to learn, in this connection, the names of the books that are held as the greatest scriptures by these followers of the Mahīmā-Dharma. These are—1, Viṣṇugarbhapurāṇa and Nirguṇa Māhātmya by Chaitaṇya Dāsa: 2, Chhattiṣā or Gupta Gītā by Balarāma Dāsa; 3, Tulābhinā by Jagannātha Dāsa and 4, Çūnya-Saṁhitā and Anādi-Saṁhita by Achyutānanda Dāsa.

BHIMA-BHOI ARAKSITADASA.

We are conscious that before proceeding further, our first and foremost duty is to give here a brief account of Bhīma Bhoi, who is not only the leader but is almost the propagator of this renascence. We find the following autobiographical sketch in his own Kali Bhāgavata :—

Born blind, Bhīma Bhoi came of the low Kanda family and first saw the light of the day in the village of Jurandā in the Dhenkānal State. His full name was Bhīma Sena Bhoi Arakṣitadāsa. He managed to earn his livelihood by husking the corn and doing other menial works for his neighbours, but he always uttered the name of the Lord, and had his mind concen-

11

trated upon His thought. And thus were passed about the first twenty-five years of his life. At length, tired of the heaviness of his life, and extremely grieved that the Lord had not yet taken pity upon his wretchedness, he determined to put an end to his life. With this end in view, he set out from his cottage and in the course of his wanderings dropped down into a well. Here he passed three days and three nights. Hearing of this, the villagers flocked to the scene of occurrence and tried to pursuade him by all the means in their power to give up the determination of sacrificing his life ; but he turned a deaf ear to all their entreaties. At length the Lord took pity upon him and at the end of the third night He assumed His own form and standing upon the brink of the well addressed Bhīma Bhoi in an affectionate tone. The latter told him of the griefs that were gnawing at his heart ; whereupon the Lord asked him to look up and behold Him. And when in obedience to this, he turned his eyes up, the born blind saw above his head, in flesh and blood, the object of his loving adoration standing in all His glory ! His whole heart was overflowing with veneration. The Lord extended His hand towards him ; he seized it firmly and in the twinkling of an eye he found himself standing side by side with his god. The Lord said, "You have obtained this interview by virtue of your prayers to me. Now I ask you to go abroad, and to publish and spread my favourite religion Alekha Dharma." He then gave him a long flowing garment called 'Kaupīna' and a belt with the following instructions, "You are to accept only alms of boiled rice for yourself. Take care that you never ask for or accept rice or anything else. And thus keeping together your body and soul with the boiled rice that you will get, you are to propagate the Mahimā-dharma." Then scrupulously following the directions of his Lord, he put on the *kaupina*, went to an adjacent village and begged alms. The owner of the house came out rice in hand, but he declined to accept this, and said "Just give me boiled rice sufficient for myself alone." The villagers heard of this, laughed at the queer idea and thought "What religion is this that aims at the abolition of the time-honoured caste-system, by making its followers live upon alms of boiled rice, irrespective of the caste or creed of the giver!" They then conferred together and determined that this new religion, a much dreaded leveller of castes, should be allowed no room whatsoever in the village. And they translated their resolution into practice by beating him off the village. Bhīma Bhoi got enraged at this, cast off his *kaupina* and belt, and proceeded towards Kapilāsa. When he had gone half way, he met with his Lord. On hearing of the intentions of Bhīma Bhoi, the latter got extremely offended and exclaimed, "You have not as yet attained *siddhi*, I suspect, or why should you take to your heels after you have been beaten?" He then bound him fast with ropes and brought him back to Jurandā; and shut him in a temple. Then all the openings were closed and he said aloud "I shall clap thrice, O Bhīma Bhoi, and, if you have attained Siddhi, you will be able to come out."

The Lord then sat down at the foot of a tree close by. He clapped thrice, and lo! Bhīma was standing before his preceptor again. At this the latter grew much pleased and said "I am satisfied now that you have attained *siddhi*. Now then I ask you to stay on in this place, to write verses about my religion and thus to spread it. You have no further need of wandering over the world." Bhīma Bhoi then married in compliance with the wishes of his preceptor and attended to all the household duties of man; but the underlying principle of his life was the propagation of his religion. To effect this he wrote several poetical works, the foremost being his Kali Bhāgavata, and composed many charming hymns (Bhajana-padāvali). In connection with our detailed treatment of the Mahimādharma hereafter, a few of these poems have been quoted *in extenso*, so we abstain from reproducing any here.

Ere long the fame of Bhīma Bhoi spread far and wide. Hearing his immortal instruction helping in the attainment of real knowledge and illumining the head and the heart, the mighty pillars of the caste system forgot themselves and stooped at his feet, though the blood of the low Kanda ran in his veins. They considered him to be a spark from the Eternal Flame of truth and knowledge and flocked around him like flies around a burning lamp. And then, before several years had elapsed, the Mahimā-dharma could count its followers by thousands. Bhīma Bhoi had heard a voice from heaven to the effect that with the revival of the Mahimā-dharma the hidden state of Jagannātha as Buddha would again be brought to light. To have this statement realised and firmly believing in it, he did now call upon his numerous disciples to come and join their forces with him. Fired with the zeal of devotion and piety, they madly obeyed his call and mustered strong under his standard. Indeed the most prominent part in the war, of which we read so much in Yaçomatī-mālikā and which, we are told, occurred in the 29th aṅka, of the reign of Divyasiṁha Deva of Puri,—the most prominent part in these wars was played by Bhīma Bhoi himself. Having equipped themselves, as best as they could, with the weapons of war, the people of about 30 villages marched upon Puri under the leadership of their preceptor. The news of their advance had already reached Puri, and the Rājā with his personal guards, was waiting to receive them duly. It was rumoured that the object of the Kumbhapaṭiā invaders was to burn the images of Jagannātha, Balarāma and Subhadrā and spread the doctrine of Nirākāra among the people of Puri. No little consternation was caused by this. But the Rājā was determined to fight to the last; and he was reinforced by a body of police officers from Pipli. No sooner had Bhīma Bhoi set his foot within the limits of Puri than both the parties fell upon one another, and a fierce fight ensued. The holy city of Puri became polluted with the blood of the heroes of both sides. At length Bhīma Bhoi became convinced of the unrealizable character of his ambition, and so proclaimed amongst his warring disciples that the avoidance from doing any harm to others was the first principle of religion; and so they should not commit sin by injuring others. He did further announce that Jagannātha had already left Puri in the guise of Buddha and he now understood that it was not Buddha's intention that his image be brought to light again. What, then, was the necessity for continuing this bloody and sinful fight? Upon this instruction falling from the lips of their leader, the Mahimā-dharmins took to flight. Some of them were, however, captured by the enemy and imprisoned, and some were transported for life on charges of murder by the British Government.* At this juncture Bhīma Bhoi declared that no true religion had ever been established without self-renunciation and self-sacrifice. So the followers of Mahimā-dharma should not mourn the loss of those who had suffered persecutions at the hands of the infidels; they should rather bless and ennoble themselves by cherishing their stainless memories.

After this, for fear of persecutions by the Government they took shelter in the hills and forests of the Gaḍajāts of Utkala.

In Yaçomatīmālikā we find the following reference to those followers of the Mahimā-dharma that were the first to embrace it or that in any way helped in propagating it :—

---

* Various false statements about this sect were made by the English and Vernacular papers of the time.

"I shall tell you, my son, the names of some of those followers who lived in the south. There is a trader in the circle of Padmapur, whose name is Hari Sāhu. He has married two girls of his own caste. You will know him easily; he is a devoted follower of mine. 193-195. In the east is Kuntibhoja bearing the name of Yogarāja. He will at first marry a girl of the Gārgara line, but she will soon pass off to that heaven which is the region of the Gandharvas. He will then marry a girl of the Simha family of Dhala-bhūma. 196-197. Inside her womb will be found, in the form of a lily, the footprints of Lakṣmī and out of that lily will be born the girl Viṣṇupriyā. When her father Yogarāja will be inspired with religious fervour, all the other devotees will also be so inspired—so great is the attachment between him and the souls of the devotees. When he will give up the ghost, he will lose himself in Brahman and will be unified with the west. The number of his

---

"दच्चिण दिगरे छन्ति येतेक भकत ।
ताङ्क नाम किछु तोते कहिबिरे सुत ॥ १९३
पद्मपुर मण्डलरे एक महाजन ।
हरिसाहु बलिण ये थिब तार नाम ॥ १९४
बिभा है थिब वेणी कन्या स्वजातिर ।
चिनिथिब वड़ भक्त घटे से आम्भर ॥ १९५
पूर्व्वे कुन्तिभोज योगराजा नाम वहि ।
प्रथमे गार्गर वंश बिभा हेब सेहि ॥ १९६
से कन्या गन्धर्व्वस्वर्गपुर चलि यिब ।
धलदेशे सिंहवंशे पुनि विभा हेब ॥ १९७

followers has completed two lacs. 198-201. I shall now tell you of him who dwells in the north. His name is Rūparāja, and he has sprung from the Kṣatriya line. 202. And now I tell you of those who live in the east. There is only one in Bengal. But there is also a king named Sabhānanda. He has married five wives with eyes like those of the gazelle. When he will marry again a girl of the Gaŋga family, he will be a devout follower of my religion and firm in his faith. 203-205. Both he and Jaya Sāhu, a Teli of the Ghāyā class, will live about the borders of Prayāga. And there are in Gaṇḍakī the great

---

लक्ष्मीङ्कर पद्मचिह्न तार गर्भे थिब ।
विष्णुप्रिया कन्या से पद्मरु जात हेब ॥ १९८
तार पिता योगराजा शुणरे नन्दन ।
से चेतिले चेतिबे आहुरि भक्तमान ॥ १९९
निज प्राण सङ्गे भक्त अटइ से टान ।
अवश्यरे रहिब थालु थिब शून्यब्रह्म ॥ २००
पश्चिम दिगरे ताकु मिशाइबे सुत ।
पूरिछन्ति प्रभुङ्कर दुइ लच भक्त ॥ २०१
उत्तर दिगरु भक्त कहि देवा शुण ।
रूपराज वलि चत्रकुलरे जनम ॥ २०२
पूर्व्वदिकै भक्त जीते कहि देवा फेड ।
एकला प्रवर्त्त ठारु बङ्गदेशे याइ ॥ २०३
सभानन्द बलिण ये एक राजा अछि ।
पांच गुठि विभा होइथिब से मृगाची ॥ २०४
ए गङ्गवंशरे विभा होइथिब येबे ।
जाणिबु से प्रभुङ्कर दृढ़भक्त तेबे ॥ २०५

hero Bhuja Sena and the devout Kamaliā Mālik, a Paṭhān by caste. 205-207.

" These seven have linked together two hundreds of thousand devoted followers. To hear this, my child, makes the mind pure and free (from lust and passion). 208. Çrīdhara of the unclean caste, Çrīkaṇṭha of the Bhoja lineage, and Keçava, Nitāi, Guṇanidhi, Mārkaṇḍa and Çrīchandana of other castes—these seven devotees have brought together two hundreds of thousand devoted followers. 209-211. These devotees will assemble themselves, male and female, in the presence of the lord, and there divert themselves by playing eternal plays with him, and their voices will be ringing in the

---

जयसाहु बलिण यै घाग्रा नामे तेलि ।
ए दुइ थिवे प्रयाग सोमान्तरे मिलि ।। २०६
गरुड़कीरे भुजसेन वड़िया पठान ।
कमलिया मल्लिकरि भक्त श्रीमान ।। २०७
दुइ लच्च भक्त ए सातकु मिशाइण ।
निर्म्मल मनरे शुणि यायरे नन्दन ।। २०८
श्रीधर वलिण यै चग्रध जातिरे ।
भोजवंशे जात इव श्रीकण्ठ नामरे । २०९
केशव निताइ गुणनिधि नामे भक्त ।
मारकण्ड श्रीचन्दन बाहुरि भकत ।। ११०
एते जन मिशिण यै दुइ लच्च भक्त ।
चेत्रपूर्व्व चटइ से डाइनिया भक्त ।। २११

twenty-one regions. 212-213. The lord will place the four Vedas in Pātāla (the infernal regions) and will introduce and establish the Çūnyadharma based upon anasādhanā." 214.

The author of Yaçomatīmālikā has, no doubt, been lavish in his praises of the heroes of his sect, but the persons, he speaks of, are not all fictitious, as is testified to by one and all of this sect. Such a hint as this has also fallen from the lips of many that there are now not only descendants of some of these great men, but that they are practically helping, though in secret, the promotion and propagation of this creed. The pioneer and leader of this sect, Bhīma Bhoi, breathed his last only ten years back. His sons are now occupying the *gadi* at Jurandā. In various parts of the Gaḍajāts one will meet with members of this community even now. But the chief *gadi* is at Jurandā near the Kapilāsa hill in the Dhenkānal State (Bhīma Bhoi used to sit here; and now it is in the occupation of his sons). The next important place is the Baḍamaṭha in the village of Golāçiŋgā within the Baud territory. It is the local belief that after he had left

एते भक्त रूण्ड हेबे प्रभुङ्क गहने।
पुरुष स्त्री मिश्रिण प्रभुङ्क सन्निधाने॥ २१२
अनन्त खेल करिबे प्रभुङ्क सङ्गरे।
शबद शोभिब ताङ्क एकइश पुरे॥ २१३
चारि वेद धर्म्म प्रभु पाताले चापिबे।
अनसाधनारे शून्यधर्म्म दीक्षा देबे॥ २१४ (यशोमतीमालिका)

the Nīlāchala, Jagannātha lived here as Buddha. Beside these, Mayūrabhañja is interspersed with maṭhas of this sect. In the villages of Kulogi, Koipur, Jaypur, Purnāpāni, Kendari and Purniā in the subdivision of Bāmanghāṭi; at Merughāṭi in Uparabhāga, in the village of Kesnā in Pānch Pir, in Upper Dihi and in the village of Gandu in Joshipur; in Navāpūrā, Puraṇā Bāripadā, Tālapadā and others in the Mayūrabhañja Proper, there is a large number of monasteries, big and small, of this sect. These maṭhas are also to be found in a large number outside Mayūrabhañja. In about 20 to 25 villages in Keonjhar, *viz.*, Sildā, Padampur, Rāŋgāmātiā, Pukhuria, Sarai &c, in almost all the Gaḍajāts such as Dhenkānāl, Baud, Dasapallā, Tālcher, Çonapur, Gāŋgpur, Pālalaharā, Rairākhol, Āthamālik, Padampur, Sāraŋgagaḍa, Rāyagaḍa, Kalāhandi, and in almost all the Killājātas, more especially in Āli, Kanikā, Bānki, Aḍang, Kujang, Sambalpur,—in all these places monasteries of this sect are to be found. The followers of this creed are divided into two classes *viz.*, Gṛhī (house-holder) and Bhikṣu or Sannyāsin. Almost wherever any large number of the followers of this sect have settled together, a small but neat and clean *matha* will attract the notice of the traveller. Amongst the Udāsinas (those who are indifferent to the ups and downs of life) only the most advanced are entitled to be the Mahānta *i.e.* the head of the monastery. Common Udāsinas or Bhikṣus find shelter in these monasteries. Amongst the members of this community, numbering not less than 25,000, there are to be found people both of the higher and lower ranks of society.

MONASTIC LIFE.

The rules that regulate their monastic life are defined with some degree of clearness in the following lines :*—

"The Sujāti (well-born Bhikṣu) will discard all family usages and give up all (religious) practices and observances, such as the performance of sacrifices and the making of burnt offerings. 148. Cutting off all connection with his wife and children, leaving behind his property and doing away with all religious vows and ceremonies, he will put on barks of kumbhi trees (kumbhipaṭa)[1] and wander about with matted hair. 149. He will sow the seed of (the religion of) Mahimā in Jambu-dvīpa and will himself be blessed by finding his spiritual preceptor, Brahman. 150. Learning the name of Anākāra Mahimā (and singing His glories) he will maintain himself by begging alms of the Nava Çudras. 151. From

* "सुजाति ये कुलधर्म्म समस्त छाड़िबे ।
होमकर्म्म याग क्रिया सकल त्यजिबे ॥ १४८
दारासुत वित्तब्रत क्रिया त्याज्य करि ।
कुम्भिपट पिन्धि फिरे थिपे जटाधरि ॥ १४९
जम्बूद्वीपे महिमाङ्क बीज से बुनिबे ।
निज ब्रह्म गुरु पाइ आनन्द लभिबे ॥ १५०
अनाकार महिमा नामकु करि भिक्षा ।
नव शूद्र घरे मागि खेलुथिबे भिक्षा ॥ १५१

(1) Hence they are called *Kumbha-Patiyā.*

Telīs, Tantris, Bhāṭas, Kerās, Rajakas, Kulārakas, Brāhmaṇas, Kṣatriyas and Chaṇḍālas, no alms are to be taken. They have been described before in the Çastras as impure. 152—153. These are of low origin and so have been marked out. 154. But the Nava Çūdras are really faithful followers of the Lord. So it is no sin to accept alms of boiled rice at their house. 155. By the great fire of the spirit of Brahman all (sins) are reduced to ashes (*i.e.* sinners are absolved); (so) he who begs alms from the house of a Çudra, commits no sin 156. * * * * *

"No other alms (than boiled rice) are to be taken from the house of the nine Çūdras. And sleep has to be enjoyed in the proper time outside the town. 160. Death resides in the sleep which is slept in the day; and boiled rice par-

---

तेली तन्ती भाठ केरा रजक कुलारक ।
ब्रह्म चेतो चण्डाल ये आबुरिला पिक ॥ १५१
एहि नव जाति घरे भिक्षा न घेनिवे ।
अशुद्ध ए माने शास्त्रे लेखियाछि पूर्ब्बे ॥ १५२
ए माने अठन्ति अधा जन्मरु जातकि ;
तेनु करि नव शूद्रे बाछि रखिछन्ति ॥ १५४
नव शूद्र अटन्ति प्रभुङ्क निज दास ।
ताङ्क घरे अन्नभिक्षा न लगाइ दोष ॥ १५५
महाब्रह्मतेजरे ये हइ याइ भस्म ।
शूद्र घरे भिक्षा कले नाहि ताङ्कु दुष्य ॥ १५६**
नव शूद्र घरे अन्न भिक्षाकु भुञ्जिवे ।
नगर बाहारे आश्र निद्राकु काटिवे ॥ १६०

taken at night is productive of evil. 161. The devotee of the Lord will take his food at day-time and pass the night without food and keep awake at dead of night. 162. * *

" Keeping awake at dead of night, you will kindle the *dhuni* (fire-pit) and thus you will be able to destroy the twenty-five causes (of creation). 230. Mutterings of prayers and set forms of meditation are useless. Only try to be indifferent (to the worldly concerns) and contemplate only the name of Mahimā." 231.

These ascetic rules (quoted from Yaçomatīmālīkā) for regulating the monastic life among the followers of Mahimā-dharma are also found to have obtained in the Buddhistic Saŋgha from very early times.

Of the twelve or thirteen ascetic rules mentioned in the Buddhistic scriptures the Mahimā-dharmin monk has even up till now been observing the rules of Piṇḍapātika,[1] Sapadāna-

---

दिवसरे निद्रा कलि काल करे बास।
रात्रे अन्नभोजन आहारे हय दोष॥ १६१
प्रभुङ्कर भक्त ये दिवसे भुञ्जिबे।
रात्रे उपवास यमकालुकु जगिबे॥ १६२
निशि उजागरे रहि धून कि जगिबु।
पञ्चिश प्रकृति तेबे पाश करिबु॥ २३०
जप नाहि तप नाहि उदासे भावरे।
एका महिमाकु नाम जपिबु हृदरे॥ २३१" (यशोमतीमालिका)

1. This is " the rule to live on food obtained by begging from door to door."

chārika,[2] Ekāsanika,[3] Pattapiṇḍika,[4] and Khalu-paççhādbhaktika;[5] but these are never found to have ever been observed by Vaiṣṇava monks or ascetics or those of any other sect. Besides, the injunction of taking alms of boiled rice from the Nava Çūdras clearly marks these Mahimā-dharmins out as quite distinct and aloof from the Vaiṣṇava or any other Hindu sect. The latter will, on no account, partake of boiled rice which has been cooked by Çudras or other low caste people.

Although Mahāyānists of the middle ages had yielded to the worship of a number of gods and goddesses, yet the Ādi Buddhists or the Hīnayānists had no faith whatsoever in the efficacy of these worships. And such is also the case with the modern Revivalists or Mahimā-dharmins. Nay, they follow the Hīnayānists more closely. As a sequel to the introduction of the worships of the sun and fire into the primitive Buddhist society, the Hīnayānists have not been able to throw off these deities altogether, though they have done away with the worships of others. And it is very interesting to note that in the Yaçomatī-mālikā of the Mahimā-dharmins, linger-

2. A rule, enjoining "a proceeding from door to door in due order when begging."

3. It enjoins "eating at one sitting."

4. It enjoins "eating from one vessel only."

5. It prohibits "the taking of a meal after it has become improper to do so; this has been interpreted as partaking of food already refused and superfluous."

Dr. Kern's Manual of Buddhism, p. 75-76.

i.g traces of this faith are also to be met with.* And just as the Buddhists of the middle ages regarded Buddha or Bodhi-sattvas as being 'Devātideva' *i. e.* God of gods, the Mahimā-dharmins also look up to Jagannātha or Buddha as being the greatest and most supreme object of worship†

We have also heard with no small surprise the essential principles of the instructions of Lerd Buddha that are known in the Buddhistic circle as Dhammapada, fall from the lips of the greatest Sannyāsins of this sect. To satisfy the curiosity of the reader, let us quote here a few

---

* "वेळो घड़ि थाव थाउ स्नान करुथिवे ।
उदे अस्त रविरङ्क दर्शन करिवे ॥ १७१
अस्त वेळे सेहि परि दृष्टि भाव याइ ।
नमस्कार करुथिवे अस्तगिरि ध्याइ ॥ १७२
अग्निदेवताकु किछि अल्प मानुथिवे ।
अन्य देव-देवी केहि किछि ना मानिवे ॥" १७३

A little before dawn you will take your bath and see both the rising and the setting of the sun. 171. Just after sunset you will fix your mind upon and bow to the Astagiri (the mountain behind which the sun was supposed to set.) 172. You should have some respect for the god of fire but not any the least respect for any other god or goddess. 173."

† "सर्व्वदेवता च बोधिसत्त्वस्य पादयोर्निपतिता। ततो राज्ञा शुद्धोदनेन बोधिसत्त्वो देवतानामप्ययं देव इति तेन बोधिसत्त्वस्य देवातिदेव इति नामधेयं कृतम् ।"

"All the gods also fell down at the feet of Bodhi-sattva. The king Suddhodana said "This Bodhi-sattva is the God of gods" and thus the name Devâtideva was given to Bodhi-sattva."

Divyâvadâna, p. 391.

couplets from the Padāvali of Bhīma Bhoi, the principal scripture of this sect.

The following song was sung by him addressing the Çūnyapuruṣa[1]—

"Though Thy body is Çūnya being destitute of all forms and colours, yet Thou hast revealed Thyself. There is there no trace of a cloud, still there are showers of water (from above); no wind, but all the forty-nine kinds of it are blowing furiously and frequently. Water is (found) flowing, though there are no rivers, and there are (also) meteoric showers. 1. There are there frequent flashes of lightning, but no one closes his eyes. In such a place is the abode of the unborn Brahman. There is here no rising or setting (of

---

(1) "शून्य-देही कन्ति उदे होइ रूप रेख नाहि हे ! (घोषा)
वरसुचि जल, नाहि मेघकुल, न थाइ पवन, उनचास बाइ वहे घन घन ।
वड़ुयछि जल, नाहि नदीकूल, उलकपात धारा होइ हे ॥ १
जक जक उदा धुकिला होइछि, कपाट न फेटू नेतरे दिसुछि,
से ठारे आश्रम अनुदित ब्रह्म, उदे अस्त नाहि तंहि हे ॥ २
वालिमाटी नाहि उबकुचि हद, गङ्गाजल छड़ि कूपजले साध,
लभिब मुकति न बुड़िब जाति, पूर्ब्ब पुण्य थिले पाइ हे ॥ ३
नियं इटा पद निष्कामे निर्ब्बेद, कल्पना ना करि धर पक्षपाद,
न वाञ्छित दषि न करा अप्र शन्यो आशा भरसा न देहि हे ॥ ४
काइ पड़िअछि नाहि वृक्षमूल, पुष्प अड़ नाहि फलिअछि फल,
फ़टिछि पतर डेम्पि नाहि तार असाधना मार्गे पाइ हे ॥ ५
पति पत्रो रूपे करन्ति युगल, इन्द्रिअन्त नाहि पिन्धिछि बकल,
से प्रभु पयरे सेव निरन्तर, भणे भीमहीन भोइ हे ॥ ६"

the sun.) 2. There is here no sand or earth and the waters of the Gaŋgā are overflowing. But if I can worship (Him) even with the waters of a well, I shall obtain salvation without losing the caste which I have come to possess through the merits of the previous life. 3. Without conceiving the Eternal Feet as attainable (only) through works done without any thought of or desire for the results and indifference (to the world), cling to the lotus-like feet (of Brahman). No need of condemning wishes and desires, no need of making one's self destitute (of all hopes and passions) and no need of giving up all hopes and expectations. 4. Shade without the tree, the fruit without the bud, and the flower and the leaf without the stalk—all these are talks of (people who follow) the way of Asādhana (non-worship). 5. He manifests Himself by creating the couple of the husband and the wife, and puts on barks of trees having no end of the senses. And so Bhīma Sena Bhoi requests all, always to worship the feet of the Lord who is so great. 6."

These lines were addressed by Bhīma Bhoi to his Guru or preceptor Buddha-svāmin.[2]—

" O Thou, that art the formless and imageless Brahman, Thou art now revealing Thyself having

---

(2) "अनाकार अरूप ब्रह्म-मूरति हे। एवे विजे करिछन्ति धरिती हे ॥ (पद)
अरूप पुरुष रूपवन्त होइले, ब्रह्माण्डकु आइले,
भकत हितकारी करुणा कृपाधारी, मायासिन्धुसागर एवे उधार करि,
पिण्डप्राणकु देइ बार भकति हे ॥ १
अगमिका पुरुष नामकु बहि, रखा निमन्ते मही,

assumed a form. Though the Formless Person, You are now possessed of a form and have come down to the world to do good to Your devotees, being full of kindness and mercy. Now be pleased to save the piṇḍaprāṇa from the ocean of māyā and fill it with devotion. 1.

"Though the Unknowable Puruṣa, You are now bearing a name for the purpose of saving the world. When a man will live upon the juice of Mahimā-dīkṣā (initiation into the Mahimā-dharma) brought about by indifference (to the world) and thus will free himself from the sins of his previous births, then will he attain, O my Lord, salvation--the end of the Virtuous. 2.

"The Indefinable Puruṣa has made himself known by coming down as a guest (as it were, into the world). The glory of Alekha is simply indefinable; He, who is the Lord of the twenty-one worlds, can be reached only through the kindness and favour of the Preceptor. 3.

"The Unimaginable Puruṣa through His imagination had limbs grown to Him. You see Him with your eyes; yet by despising Him who

---

निर्ब्वेंद रु प्रकाश, महिमा दीचा रस, भजि येवे पारिव जीव पूर्ब्ब कल्मष,

तेवे पाइव सदगति मुकति हे ॥२

अचिह्न पुरुष से ये चिह्निवा देलि, आपे अतिथि हेलि,

अलेख पद जेहु लेखि न होइ सेहु, गुरु पणे भकता भटग्ति महावाहु,

एकइश भुवने सेहु नृपति हे ॥३

अकल्पन पुरुष से कल्पन कले, अङ्ग सर्ब्बे जनमिले,

is it that you are worshipping? Know that this world is still existing only because there is the Mahimā-dharma. 4.

"The Imperishable Puruṣa, He is never to perish; and not only He, but Guruvīja and the disciple, these two also are never to perish. All the days do pass in great bliss, the very sight of Guru destroying all evils. 5.

"In this dark Kaliyuga He has revealed Himself to the world, having assumed a form. Save this there is not a single word, so grand, so sweet and so capable of redemption. With great humility does Bhīma Arakṣita bow down at the feet of the Lord, which can confer emancipation. 6."

INCARNATION OF BUDDHA.

We have now been able, we hope, to establish the fact that the Mahimā-dharmins of the Gaḍajāts of Orissa are simply Buddhists. Like other Buddhists of the Mahāyāna School, they are also passing their days in the firm belief and hope that Buddha will again be incarnated. We

---

आन से करतांकु नेवरे देखु देखु, निन्दित करु अच्छ भजुअच्छ काहाकु,
एवं महिमा-धर्म्म थाक पारिथि है ॥ ४
अक्षय पुरुष क्षय हेबाकु नाहि, एकु नहि दुइ ब्रह्माण्डे गुरुवीजे शिष्य नाहान्ति केहि
बड़ हि मा पणे सर्व्वे दिन याउछि हि, गुरुदर्शने खण्ड काल विपति है ॥ ५
देहधारी होइछन्ति महीमण्डले, ए घोर कलिकाले,
एबना एकाक्षर नाहि वीरवर, वचन सुधाधार मुक्तिदानी पयर,
भणे भीम अरक्षित करि विनति है ॥ ६"

could not do better than quote the following few lines from their Yaçomatīmālīkā to show their belief in the incarnation of Buddha and the real nature of their creed—

"चाहि कलिमध्यरे भकते छन्ति रहि ।
बुद्ध अवतार रुप दर्शन ना पाइ ॥ १७७
विहारमण्डले शून्यगादि तुलाइवे ।
से अलेख प्रभु धुनिकुण्ड गुप्त थिवे ॥ १७८
मायारुपे बुद्ध अवतारे नरदेही ।
भक्तजन हिते भक्त उद्धारिबें पाइ ॥ १७९"

"In the Kaliyuga the devotees are passing their lives in disguise, though they have not yet seen the form of the incarnation of Buddha, in the hope that the *gadi* (seat) of the Çūnya will be established in the province of Behar and there the Lord Alekha will lie concealed in the Dhunikuṇḍa (fire-pit). The Alekha will through His creative power, assume the form of a human being in the incarnation of Buddha for the good of His devotee, who will thus attain emancipation".

*INDEX.**

* The figures in italics indicate the pages of Introduction.